JACK LONDON

ADVENTURES, IDEAS,

AND FICTION

Literature and Life: American Writers

Complete list of titles in the series available from the publisher on request.

JACK LONDON

ADVENTURES,

IDEAS,

AND FICTION

James Lundquist

UNGAR · NEW YORK

1987
The Ungar Publishing Company
370 Lexington Avenue, New York, N.Y. 10017

Printed in the United States of America

Library of Congress Cataloging-in-Publication Data

Lundquist, James.
  Jack London, adventures, ideas, and fiction.

  (Literature and life. American writers)
  Bibliography: p.
  Includes index.
  1. London, Jack, 1876–1916.   2. Authors,
American – 20th century – Biography.   3. Adventure
and adventurers – United States – Biography.
I. Title.   II. Series.
PS3523.O46Z764   1987   818'.5209   [B]   86-28052
ISBN 0-8044-2566-3

Contents

Chronology

1876   Jack London is born January 12 in San Francisco.
His mother, Flora Wellman, names William Henry
Chaney, an itinerant "professor of astrology," as the
father. On September 7 Flora marries John Lon-
don, a widower with two daughters, Eliza and Ida.
Flora names her son John Griffith London.

1891   London finishes grammar school in Oakland after
a childhood spent living in a dreary succession of
flats, rented houses, and small farms in the East Bay
area. Works in cannery, purchases sloop (the *Razzle Dazzle*), becomes an oyster pirate and then an in-
formal member of the California Fish Patrol.

1893   Sails to North Pacific and Japan on the seal-hunting
Sophia Sutherland, January to August. On November
12 wins first prize in a San Francisco *Morning Call*
writing contest for "Story of a Typhoon off the Coast
of Japan."

1894   Leaves in April on an eight-month cross-country
trip as a tramp. Serves thirty-day sentence in July
for vagrancy at Erie County Penitentiary, New
York.

1895   Attends Oakland High School and writes for student magazine, *The High School Aegis*.

1896   Quits high school and studies for University of California entrance examinations. Joins Socialist Labor
Party. Enrolls at Berkeley for the fall semester.

1897   Withdraws from Berkeley because of financial
        problems. Begins speaking for socialist causes
        while trying to establish career as a writer. Sails for
        the Klondike and spends the winter in the Yukon.
        Stepfather dies.

1898   Floats down the Yukon River to the Bering Sea.
        Returns home in August and begins writing his
        Northland stories. *Overland Monthly* accepts "To the
        Man on Trail" in December.

1899   *Overland Monthly* publishes several more Northland
        stories. *Atlantic Monthly* accepts "An Odyssey of the
        North."

1900   Marries Bess Maddern on April 7. Houghton Mif-
        flin publishes his first book of stories, *The Son of the
        Wolf.*

1901   Daughter, Joan, is born January 15. Finishes *A
        Daughter of the Snows* in March.

1902   Sails for England in July to collect material for *People
        of the Abyss* in London's East End. Daughter, Bess,
        is born October 20. First novel, *The Cruise of the
        Dazzler,* is published by Century. Second novel, *A
        Daughter of the Snows,* is published by J. B. Lippin-
        cott. Returns home in mid-November and begins
        The Call of the Wild.

1903   Separates from wife after beginning a love affair
        with Charmian Kittredge. *The Call of the Wild* is
        published by Macmillan and brings him interna-
        tional fame.

1904   Completes *The Sea-Wolf* in January. Travels to Ja-
        pan and Korea to report the Russo-Japanese War
        for the Hearst press. Returns in June.

1905   Buys 130-acre Hill ranch near Glen Ellen in Sonoma County, California, in spring. Completes *White Fang*. Travels through the Midwest and East on a socialist lecture tour. Divorced in November; marries Charmian Kittredge on November 19 in Chicago.

1906   Completes lecture tour in February. Reports San Francisco earthquake for *Collier's*. Finishes *The Iron Heel* and begins building his famous ketch, the *Snark*.

1907   Visits Hawaii, the Marquesas, and Tahiti on the *Snark*. Works on *Martin Eden*.

1908   Returns home on steamship *Mariposa* to work out financial problems and then continues cruise on the *Snark* in the South Seas. Suffers from malaria, yaws, and a variety of tropical diseases and ailments.

1909   Hospitalized in Sydney, Australia, and abandons plans to sail the *Snark* around the world. Returns to California via South America on the freighter *Tymeric*. Arrives home in August.

1910   Completes *Burning Daylight*. Starts construction of his mansion, Wolf House, on ranch. Daughter, Joy, is born June 19 and dies thirty-eight hours later.

1911   Drives four-horse carriage across northern California and southern Oregon with Charmian.

1912   Sails around Cape Horn from Baltimore aboard the *Dirigo* with Charmian. Second baby is lost through miscarriage. Writes *John Barleycorn*.

1913   Begins writing *The Star Rover*. Wolf House destroyed by fire (arson suspected).

1914   Goes to Mexico in April to report the Mexican

Revolution for *Collier's*. Returns with severe dysentery and acute pleurisy.

1915   Goes to Hawaii to regain health. Works on final South Seas stories. Returns to Glen Ellen in July and leaves again for Hawaii in December.

1916   Returns to Glen Ellen for the last time in August. Suffers from uremia and rheumatism. On November 22 dies of gastrointestinal uremia and self-administered morphine.

JACK LONDON

1

The Brain Merchant

"This is almost the rawest edge of the world," Jack London wrote in 1908 from the Solomon Islands during his voyage to the South Seas aboard his forty-five-foot ketch the *Snark*. Head-hunting, cannibalism, and murder were so rampant among the natives on the worst islands that London had to maintain constant night watches and went armed twenty-four-hours a day. London told of being attacked by headhunters when the *Snark* hung up on a reef. Writing with obvious relish, London related how half his crew held off the bushmen with rifles while the other half worked to save the vessel.[1] London's wild and woolly account details but one of many adventures he packed into his forty years — adventures that included shipping before the mast on a sealing expedition to the Bering Sea, rambling across the country as a hobo, climbing the Chilkoot Pass to reach the gold fields of the Klondike, disappearing into the most notorious slums of England to write a firsthand account of the sordid life lived there, riding through dangerous territory on horseback in Korea to cover the Russo-Japanese War, and going to Veracruz to write about the Mexican Revolution.

London was always ready to travel to the "raw edges" of the world, and much of the power in his writing derives directly from the risks he took. But every one of his adventures was fueled by ideas that came out of his reading, out of his constant search for a personal philosophy of life that would make sense of his raw experiences and enable him to go after his dreams with a big stick and club them to death. He took tremendous chances, and it was as if he had unconsciously adopted the name of his favorite Oakland bar—Johnny Heinold's First and Last Chance Saloon—as his motto. His life was short and often desperate, crammed with outrageous drinking bouts and sudden departures to distant wars; yet he was one of our most literate writers, self-educated in the best American tradition, and the night watches that Jack London kept were more often over books than over cannibals.

This, of course, is not the image Jack London projected to his public. Adventurer, revolutionist, voice of the proletariat, a writer of he-man fiction, a true hero (who had proved himself again and again shooting the White Horse Rapids while thousands of Klondike trekkers cheered from the cliffs above), an expert on boxing, sailing, bicycling, fishing, and duck hunting—this is the image his readers demanded, and in a sense he was all it represented. Despite many attempts to debunk his legend, London was not a faker. It is doubtful that one could find another writer—not even Hemingway—who led such a truly adventurous, genuinely courageous life. So attractive and so profitable was his reputation that at the height of his fame he was plagued by doubles who traveled the country trying to pass themselves off as Jack London.[2] London achieved something of the status of a folk hero in his own time, and he has pretty much remained an emblematic figure ever since.

But there were many dimensions to London's adventuresome spirit. His lust for excitement was accompanied by violent appetites and compulsions that drove him from one extreme to another. He loved to gorge himself on "cannibal sandwiches" of raw beef and onions on the Oakland waterfront, and during the duck season he sometimes lived on two blood-red canvas-backs a day. He wrote a book, *John Barleycorn*, that advocated Prohibition, but he would often drink a quart of whiskey in an afternoon, and once, according to his own admission, stayed drunk for twenty-one days straight. He preached socialism and revolution, but usually traveled with an Oriental valet who was literally expected to wait on his master hand and foot — even down to tying his shoelaces. London fancied himself the hero of the working man, and was generous to a fault with the money he made, but he was equally capable of pouring thousands of dollars into the *Snark*, into his ranch in the Valley of the Moon north of San Francisco, and into his mansion, Wolf House. Even though he was accident-prone throughout his life, repeatedly getting kicked by horses or thrown from them, and one time nearly drowning after falling off an Oakland wharf while drunk, London struggled to maintain a Californian's dream of physical prowess, lordly physique, and eternal youth.

London also liked to trade on the story of his rags-to-riches success, stressing the miseries he had to endure as a child, claiming that he did not own a store-bought shirt until he was eight years old, and that as a lad in school he was so hungry that he stole meat from a little girl's lunch bucket. In his autobiographical writings London depicts himself struggling against incredible odds as he recounts the ferocity with which he sought success amid the rejection slips that piled up around his desk when he made his first attacks on the literary marketplace. And in describing his adventures, he portrays himself as one man alone battling with tremendous endurance against the enormous powers of nature. Here, for example, is the Jack London glimpsed in the foreword to *The Cruise of the Snark*: "About me are the great natural forces — colossal menaces, Titans of destruction, unsentimental monsters that have less concern for me than I have for the grain of sand I crush under my feet."

London could get away with such self-adulation because of the strong impression he made on most of the people he met. Many testified again and again to his magnetism and power, some saying in all seriousness that at times he appeared to be radiating light, almost as if there were an aura of electricity about him. "He is one of the most approachable of men," wrote a reporter in a somewhat less worshipful vein in 1903, "unconventional, responsive and genuine, with a warmth of hospitality which places the visitor on the immediate footing of a friend. In fact, Jack London, boyish, noble, and lovable, is made up of qualities that reach straight for the heart."[3] It is this impression of energy, youthfulness, openness, and general good humor that shows up in most descriptions of the writer.

Even in his final days, when he was bloated, sick, and in great pain, London was able to display optimism and surprising humor. Down to the end he was thinking of new books that he fully intended to write, including a series of essays that would expose modern self-delusion and advocate individual nobility and self-sacrificing love. To be certain, another side is revealed in a novel he actually started shortly before his death. Its title was to be *How We Die*, and in it he wanted to deal subjectively and pitilessly with five stories of men dying, depicting each of them wrestling with disillusionment. "And now," a dying sea captain reflects on his life, "when he had grown to care for it; when he cherished and cuddled it — ran no risks, behold, it was fading, failing, oozing away from the mass of helpless wreckage that had once been his body, fleshed and filled with the heady stuff of life."[4] Dark as this projected novel is, one phrase stands out — "the heady stuff of life" — because it is this exuberance that formed the core of Jack London's personality and work. This comes through in one of the last memoirs of London the adventurer. Ford Madox Ford was with London in Tampico in 1914 during the Mexican Revolution. He remembered a darkly Celtic Jack London with flashing eyes, surprisingly full of energy, and stirred to boyish excitement over a revolver fight in a saloon. Ford saw him as a man who seemed constitutionally unable to grow up, a writer who insisted in telling his own stories with such enthusiasm that he ended up believing them himself.[5]

So good are London's stories about himself and so fascinating is his life that he was the subject of enormous publicity while he lived, and seven full biographies have been published in English since his death. Each of the biographies, in one way or another, depicts London as a brooding genius whose spectacular rise from the Oakland streets to world fame was offset by his inability to make a mature adjustment to the grim facts of his origins and his early environment. London himself did much to make the job of a biographer difficult, and his lifelong tendency to fictionalize himself in his remarkable autobiographical works has encouraged his biographers to make use of some too obviously dramatic possibilities in working up narrative accounts of his life.[6]

London's discovery at age twenty-one that John London was not his father, and that he most likely was the bastard son of William H. Chaney, an itinerant astrologer, is generally taken to be the most traumatic factor in the development of his personality and his artistic consciousness. This concept is set forth in Irving Stone's 1938 "biographical novel" *Sailor on Horseback*, and is more or less supported by subsequent biographers. The theory does have some substance. Many of London's stories and several of his novels do present themes that could be grouped under the heading of "illegitimacy": the idea of the exiled hero who, for all his strength, power, and independence, seems to have no legitimate heritage, and in the end must succeed or fail in facing up to his isolation from others. There are some problems, however, with such an approach to the London biography. These themes are only a few among many in London's work. But more important, the stigma of illegitimacy was simply not quite as great in the Oakland and San Francisco of London's youth as his chroniclers have made it out to be. San Francisco, the place of his birth, was a city where unmarried partners lived together openly, and London could not have helped knowing about the uncertain origins of many of the people he met while growing up in the Bay area. At the very least, there is little evidence that he questioned his legitimacy while he was a boy. If anything, it was his bookishness that set him apart from his schoolmates, although he seems to have made an early adjustment to the tough scenes of his childhood and indeed thrived so well that by the time he was sixteen he was a notorious figure in the saloons of the Barbary Coast. At no time in his subsequent life does the truth about his father detract from the colorful, wonderfully appealing figure of Jack London that his public loved. That London went through inner tortures because of what he learned about William H. Chaney cannot be doubted; that he got over them in fairly good shape has not been stressed often enough.

Whatever problems the truth about his lineage caused him, London went on to become the "Father of Red-Blooded American Literature," and he remains something of a fantasy figure in the popular imagination, envisaged as a hard-drinking musher in a fur parka driving a dog sled through the white silence of the far north. Indeed, a high-proof concoction of blended Canadian whiskey, Yukon Jack, owes no small debt for its success to this aspect of London's fame. But many contemporary accounts depict London quite differently. Marshall Bond, one of London's acquaintances in the Klondike, for instance, described a discussion of socialism that took place one winter night in a cabin on the Yukon River. London was sitting on a box, out of the circle of light from the lamp, and when the argument stalled on a difficult point, he spoke up from the shadows, tracing the subject from its earliest history and effectively ending the debate. "Intellectually he was incomparably the most alert man in the room, and we felt it," Bond wrote. "Some of us had minds as dull as putty and some of us had been educated and drilled into the goose step of conventionalism. Here was a man whose life and thoughts were his own. He was refreshing. This was my first introduction to Jack London."[7]

London had little formal education—he did not graduate from high school and he spent only one term as a special student at the University of California—but he was an omnivorous reader and acquired a range of knowledge so impressive that when his essay "What Life Means to Me" appeared in *Cosmopolitan* in March 1906, the New York *Independent* reported, "We have had many ambitious studies of American life, from Tocqueville to Munsterberg, but not one of them has penetrated so deeply into the heart of it as does the frank self-revelation of an American gifted with the divine fire, who has intensely lived it."[8] In giving an account of his working-class background and the development of his socialist beliefs, London stresses in the essay that it was his view of "the pit, the abyss, the human cesspool, the charnel house of our civilization" that made reading immediately relevant to him. Living among cutthroats and thieves, he was "scared into thinking," scared into beginning a "frantic pursuit of knowledge" that would make him what he termed a "brain merchant." And whatever his audience wanted to think of him as being, that is how London, in his most honest moments, came

to think of himself—as a writer, and a "brain merchant," whose often brutal and terrifying experiences
had been given redemptive meaning through the vehe-
ment ideologies he constructed out of the thousands of
books he read and annotated. He read Spencer,
Darwin, Mill, Marx, Nietzsche, and even Freud and
Jung. He studied Kipling, laboriously copying the British writer's stories out in longhand to get a better feel
for the cadences. He was devoted to Mark Twain and
Bret Harte. He was the first major American writer of
fiction to take Herman Melville seriously, and he wrote
The Sea-Wolf with *Moby-Dick* in mind.

London was influenced by all of these writers and
by hundreds of others but he was never entirely dominated by any of them. There was too much of the intellectual hobo in London for that. He roamed far and
wide for his ideas, and he took handouts where he
could get them; but he knew that if he were to travel
fast and sure he would have to discard all but the stuff
that would actually work when he wanted it to. What
resulted was a kind of fiction that is not so much
stripped down as it is tightly packed with a few good
ideas, drawn sometimes from the most unlikely sources
and embedded in a situation or event London understood firsthand. His stories do drip blood-red, his
wolves grab for the jugular, and the howls of beasts
echo through his pages. But behind it all is an unstated
purpose: "I was scared into thinking," Jack London
said, and he always wanted the same thing to happen to
his readers.

"A very loose condition of society was fashionable at
San Francisco at the time," wrote Jack London's father, William H. Chaney, concerning 1876, the year of
London's birth. And in the same letter to his son,
whom he never acknowledged, Chaney added that "it
was not thought disgraceful for two to live together
without marriage."¹ San Francisco at the time was a city

made up of unattached transients, many of whom had
been drawn by the Gold Rush, others simply by the
free-and-easy social climate where "Men drank too
much, the divorce rate was scandalous, and supposedly
proper circles admitted too many of the compromised
into their ranks."[10] It was a city where one could hear
derelict ideas and manic philosophies argued and displayed everywhere by the diverse population of what,
in its nineteenth-century remoteness, was a city-state of
hills, fog, and sudden, superb views of the Bay and the
Golden Gate. There were the dens of Chinatown and
the splendid isolation of Telegraph Hill; and literary
visitors such as Robert Louis Stevenson and Oscar
Wilde were attracted by what seemed to them to be the
only place where Peking and Marseilles could be sam-
pled at the same time.

San Francisco was exotic, full of contradictions,
teeming with eccentrics, and possessed of a prodigal
craziness into which Jack London was born at 615
Third Street on the twelfth of January. His place of
birth, London was later to write, "incontinently intermingled its slums and mansions as did the old cities of
Europe. Nob Hill arose, like any medieval castle, from
the mess and ruck of common life that denned and
laired at its base."[11] But out of this turmoil of poverty,
Bohemianism, and generalized vice arose a violent radicalism peddled at first by disappointed placer miners,
revivalists, escapees from Eastern mental institutions,
reformers of the currency, casual murderers from the
Barbary Coast, proto-socialists out of Eastern jails, and
cranks of every stripe. This was the San Francisco to
which London's parents — his father a "professor" of astrology and his mother a spiritualist — migrated, and
where, for a while at least, they felt right at home with the
other strange breeds that gravitated and levitated their
way across the philosophical and theological wilderness
of America, seeking the golden gate of illumination.

They were a weird couple and much has been

written about the dismal circumstances of London's birth, but in many respects his parents were fascinating people, who illustrated in their tortured and chaotic lives the elements of dissatisfaction and emancipation that can be seen in such diverse contemporaries as Mark Twain and Emily Dickinson, and that showed up in movements ranging from Theosophy to the Salvation Army. "The intellectual ferment of the times, at work in a new, rapidly expanding country that was culturally isolated to a great extent from the rest of the world, expressed itself in curious ways," writes London's daughter, Joan, in her biography of her father, *Jack London and His Times*. "Any cause whose appeal was either humanitarian, pseudoscientific or religious, or which promised freedom from old beliefs and restraints, found enthusiastic followers."[12] The forces of revolt often joined hands with the revolt against the old faith, and "professors" of phrenology and "astrophysiology" wandered across the United States politicizing as well as preaching their various revelations. Many of these people were fools whose own doctrines often wore them out and destroyed their lives through their years of excommunication and ridicule; but what most of them sought was indeed accomplished — the nature of American society itself was permanently altered.

Jack London's mother should be included in this group. Flora Wellman was a believer in spiritualism and earned part of her living holding séances and giving lectures on the spirit world. She believed that the dead survive as spirits on an "astral plane," and that they could communicate with the living through the help of a third party, a "medium," which she believed herself to be.

The practice of spiritualism took many forms, some sensational and some almost scientific. It was virtually unknown in the United States until 1848, when there were some odd happenings at the house of a farmer named Fox in upstate New York. For a long time the occupants of the house had been disturbed by knocking and rattling noises at night. Fox's youngest daughter, Kate, challenged the supposed ghost to repeat a certain sequence of "rappings" and managed to establish a code through which the spirit identified himself as a man who had been murdered in the house. The "Fox Case" received so much attention that the practice of conducting séances (literally, "sittings" in French) turned into a national mania; and Kate and her two sisters spent much of their later lives acting as mediums in the United States and England. Because it seemed to be a religion based not on ancient tradition but on observable phenomena, spiritualism offered a new faith for those who could no longer accept Christianity. It also provided new hope of immortality for those whose materialistic ways of thinking had made the idea of life after death impossible to accept.

Far from being a crank movement as we might think it, spiritualism received serious attention from nearly all the intellectuals of the time. In 1872, for example, Harriet Beecher Stowe conducted a correspondence across the ocean with George Eliot concerning a conversation Mrs. Stowe had carried on with the shade of Charlotte Brontë by means of a *planchette*, an automatic writing device that wrote messages when moved involuntarily by hands placed on it. Eliot found the message itself to be improbable, but did not dismiss spiritualism as a serious consideration in itself. "I would not willingly place any barrier between my mind and any possible channel of truth affecting the human lot,"[13] she wrote.

Flora Wellman got an early introduction to spiritualism in her hometown, Massillon, Ohio, where the "Abby Warner Case," one of the most famous incidents in the history of the movement, took place when Flora was eight years old. Abby Warner was a medium who monitored the rappings of spirits in the presence of the congregation of St. Timothy's Episcopal Church on Christmas Eve 1851, and she was charged with having willfully disturbed a Christian assembly engaged in the solemnity of worship. No proof could be brought forth against her and she was not convicted, but, as in the earlier instance of the Fox sisters, the incident generated tremendous controversy. How much immediate influence Abby Warner had on Flora is difficult to say, but at sixteen she ran away from home and little is known about her travels or how she earned a living until she surfaced at thirty-one in San Francisco with William H. Chaney, a self-taught lawyer who was born near Chesterville, Maine, in 1821.

Like the spiritualism practiced by Flora, the astrology preached by Chaney was a serious concern of the times, particularly in San Francisco, where the Board of Supervisors tried to control the activities of astrologers, fortune-tellers, and clairvoyants in the 1870s by ordering a licensing fee of fifty dollars per quarter. Chaney regarded astrology as both an exact science and a religion that could be understood through the principles of "Astrotheology." Chaney was well known as a writer, and not only in astrological pamphlets and magazines. He contributed articles to *Common Sense, a Journal of Live Ideas*, edited in San Francisco by the journalist William Slocum and described as

a magazine in which political radicalism rubbed shoulders with every other kind of unorthodoxy — free love, diet reform, spiritualism, and astrology. There was a considerable overlap among these veins of thought, and the general feeling that they were all subversive of tradition and the established order led their enthusiasts to support one another and to receive Chaney favorably in their circles.[14]

Chaney was very much a part of the intellectually rebellious mood of his era, and for a time at least he was taken seriously as a spokesman for beliefs so radical and dangerous that he once was imprisoned for twenty-eight weeks in Ludlow Street prison in New York following an astrology meeting that had been broken up by hoodlums. He was an excellent speaker, a powerful opponent in debate, and wrote stories and novels (now unfortunately lost). "Although Chaney was not above taking advantage of favorable circumstances to make a living out of astrology," Joan London writes, "he would have indignantly rejected any dismissal of his science as quackery. He studied constantly both the mechanics and theory of his subject, and earnestly believed that astrology could be a most powerful factor for bettering the world by ensuring the breeding and raising of superior human beings."[15]

But for all of Chaney's visionary pronouncements, practicing what he preached was another matter when Flora announced in 1875 that she was pregnant. He demanded that she get an abortion. When she refused, he insisted that she pack up and leave the house at 122 First Avenue in San Francisco, where they had been living. Flora's subsequent suicide attempt (she tried to shoot herself with a revolver after first taking laudanum) made the headlines in the San Francisco *Chronicle* for June 4, 1875, and the scandal was so great that Chaney's career and reputation in California were effectively ruined. He deserted Flora, went to the Northwest, later lived a long time in Chicago, and died well over eighty years old, just as Jack London was enjoying his first real success with the publication of *The Call of the Wild*.

One of the ironies among many in Jack London's life is that he invented several stories about his lineage to cover up the facts of his ancestry, all the while failing to understand that his parents, at least, were truly remarkable people. His mother was a fiercely independent woman who led a life of relentless defiance, refusing to give up her belief in spiritualism, and even refusing to buckle under to her son when he became famous and tried to get her to cover up what he presumed to be her eccentricities. And his father was a man who, had he perhaps enjoyed more favorable circumstances — or a better horoscope — might have turned out to be more than a curious footnote in the biography of his son. As it is, the birthdays of father and son are only a day apart: January 13 for Chaney, January 12 for London. And both had Saturn in evil aspect to Libra — good, but dangerous, for the creation of genius.

Jack London was born in the home of Mrs. Amanda Slocum, who had earlier befriended Flora and who was superintendent of the Woman's Publishing Company, a successful book and job-printing business on Montgomery Street. The birth had been difficult for Flora, and in her weakened condition she was not able to feed her son. A black woman, Jennie Prentiss, who had been born a slave in Virginia and who had recently lost her own child, was employed as a wet nurse. Mrs. Prentiss was to remain an influence in Jack London's life for years, and her steadiness provided him with the kind of emotional refuge that his mother could never afford him as she tried to make a living giving music lessons and lecturing on spiritualism. The relationship with Mrs. Prentiss also provided Flora with something else: an introduction to John London, a middle-aged widower who had come to California with two of his seven children and who had found work with Jennie Prentiss's husband, a building contractor. On September 7, 1876, Flora and John London were married in San Francisco, and John London gave Flora's son his name.

John and Flora were anything but a perfect match, but for a time he did take an interest in her spiritualism; and however much his retiring nature clashed with her willfulness, he was kind to Jack. John London had worked as a carpenter, a sewing machine salesman, and a handyman, and operated a small grocery store at Seventh and Campbell Street in Oakland during Jack's early years. He was devoted to Jack and willingly acknowledged him as his son, but John London had suffered from lung trouble ever since the Civil War and soon descended into the role of a long-suffering husband having to put up with his wife's séances and temper tantrums. He spent his last years (he died in 1897) as a night watchman and special constable, but he was by no means a weak influence on his stepson. Jack's boyhood friend Frank Atherton later said that John London often entertained the boys with stories about the Indian wars and was known on the waterfront as a fearless constable.

John London was also a drinking man, and often took young Jack along with him to the bar. Writing in *John Barleycorn* about his life at age seven when the family moved to a potato ranch in San Mateo County south of San Francisco, London remembered that "the brightest spots in my child life were the saloons. Sitting on the heavy potato wagons, wrapped in fog, feet stinging from inactivity, the horses plodding slowly along the deep road through the sandhills, one bright vision was the saloon at Colma, where my father, or whoever drove, always got out to get a drink."

Jack London himself was destined to be a saloonman virtually from that time on, testifying in *John Barleycorn* that he was five years old the first time he got drunk, and that at seven he once drank so much wine that he imagined he was pursuing his father through the whorehouses and gambling dens in San Francisco's Chinatown. "In my delirium I wandered deep beneath the ground through a thousand of these dens, and behind locked doors of iron I suffered and died a thousand deaths," London writes concerning this incident,

And when I would come upon my father, seated at table in these subterranean crypts, gambling with Chinese for great stakes of gold, all my outrage gave vent in the vilest cursing. I would rise in my bed, struggling against the detaining hands, and curse my father till the rafters rang. All the inconceivable filth a child running at large in a primitive countryside may hear men utter, was mine; and though I had never dared utter such oaths, they now poured from me, at the top of my lungs, as I cursed by father sitting there underground and gambling with long-haired, long-nailed Chinamen.[16]

The seventies and eighties were depression years in California, and the London family once was forced to move five times in as many years. One of Jack London's earliest memories was of being left alone at the age of three in a house from which they were in the process of moving. "The quietness of the dismantled room, the grotesque piles of furniture and boxes of household goods oppressed him with a sense of desolation that quickly turned to fear," Joan London explains. "In the yard next door a woman was beating carpets. To the frightened child the monotonous whacking was the only familiar thing in a suddenly alien world. He clung to it, listening with all his ears, but after a while the noise ceased and silence closed in about him completely. It seemed more dreadful to try to escape than to remain, but summoning all his courage, he clenched his fists and fled."[17]

The inevitable insecurity Jack London experienced eventually gave way to an indifference toward close family ties. His mother's obsession with business schemes — selling gold leaf for picture-framing, founding a kindergarten, dealing in lottery tickets — is understandable given the hard times, but her unwillingness to spend much time with her son meant that Jack's care was essentially turned over to his stepsister, Eliza, six years older (and it was Eliza who years later became his most trusted business advisor and manager). But however erratic his mother's behavior became, she was trying to improve the family's fortunes as best she could, and London did not lack food, clothing, or even such luxuries as trips to the circus with his stepfather when he was a young boy.

Most important of all, however, was that he had access to books. His mother was interested in ideas (however strange they may seem to us now), and believed in the importance of reading, if not of formal education, as a way to unlock the mysteries of the spirit world into which she had flung herself. And her willingness to entrust the mothering of Jack to Eliza only encouraged his early devotion to reading. When the family lived at Alameda, Eliza took little Jack to school with her and the teacher provided him with a box for a desk, drawing materials, and picture books. Eliza often read to him in the evenings, and later said that he begged her for more and more stories and that as soon as he was able to read on his own he always seemed to have a book in his hands.

In *John Barleycorn* London mentions four books among the earliest he can recall reading. Two, Paul du Chaillu's African travels and Washington Irving's *Alhambra*, with its vivid picture of Spain, fired a passion for the distant and exotic. But the other two, Ouida's *Signa* and Horatio Alger's *From Canal Boy to President*, had more immediate influence. Ouida (actually the pen name for Marie Louise de la Ramée) was an immensely popular writer; her *Signa* is about an Italian peasant boy who overcomes the loss of his mother and survives the harsh treatment of an uncle to become a famous violinist. Although London said that the last forty pages of his copy of the book were missing, the happy ending of the rags-to-riches story was apparent enough to him in his own circumstances, which he took to be similar to Signa's. "For genius is fanaticism," Ouida wrote, "and the barefoot hungry fellow running errands in the dust, had genius in him, and was tossed about by it like a small moth by a storm."[18] *From Canal*

Boy to President, a biography published shortly after James A. Garfield's assassination in 1881, develops a theme that appears in almost all of Alger's books: the idea that poverty is no bar to success, and that through hard work, honesty, and a little luck, combined with a determination to improve, even the most ignorant and ragged youth could achieve reasonable, if not always spectacular, success. Jack London, along with many other boys of his age, devoured Alger's stories and turned them into a gospel of practicality.

London's passionate interest in books was furthered in 1886 when the family moved back to Oakland and he gained access to the public library, a run-down wooden building next to the old City Hall on Fourteenth Street, where cards were obtained for every member of the family.

London maintained his reading habits as best he could, despite having to begin work at age ten in a series of jobs as newsboy, helper on an ice wagon, pinsetter in a bowling alley, and saloon sweeper. All of his money was then turned over to his mother. After graduating from grammar school at thirteen, he went to work at Hickmott's Cannery, often working eighteen hours a day (including at least one thirty-six-hour stretch) stuffing pickles into jars for ten cents an hour. As London testifies concerning this time, in *John Barleycorn*, "I asked myself if this were the meaning of life — to be a work-beast? I knew of no horse in the city of Oakland that worked the hours I worked. If this were living, I was entirely unenamored of it."

His life was harsh, but not unusual for a proletarian youth in those days when few Americans even attended high school, and the folk heroes were men such as Andrew Carnegie, John D. Rockefeller, and (later) Henry Ford, whose early prospects were not much brighter than were London's. And there were other compensations. London was able to save enough money to buy a fourteen-foot, decked-over skiff equipped with centerboard and sail, and take it out on the Oakland Estuary, where he could mingle with ships from all over the world, as well as with the smaller craft manned by fishermen, trash hunters, and smugglers. He also was able to find his way into a dangerous life that, in a harshly dramatic way, gave an extra edge to the tales of romance and adventure he had been reading. "I belonged to a 'street gang' in West Oakland, as rough and tough a crowd as you'll find in any city in the country," he recalled.[1] With other members of the gang, he was in and out of saloons, associated with roistering sailors and the waterfront, and drifted into a life of petty crime that soon suggested a grander scheme: to become an oyster pirate.

It is at this point that it becomes difficult to separate fact from fiction in recounting Jack London's life, because his career as an oyster pirate was the first of a series of adventures from which he drew the essential stuff of his fiction. The primary source of information concerning this and other adventures — the seven-month sealing voyage on the *Sophia Sutherland*, the tramping experiences of 1894, the famous expedition to the Yukon during the Klondike gold rush in 1897–98, the six weeks spent in the lower depths of London's East End in 1902, the nearly fatal experiences in Korea while on assignment as a correspondent for the Hearst newspapers in 1904 during the Russo-Japanese War, and the ill-fated "world cruise" aboard the *Snark*, 1907–1909 — is London himself, and this makes for some obvious problems. But the adventures did occur, and however exaggerated London's subsequent accounts of them are, they kept his imagination stoked for years.

As much as these adventures contributed to the London legend, they were not simply the raw experiences of youth; at every point, virtually in every incident, Jack London viewed his experiences against a background of ideas that he had developed out of his constant reading. At first it was Ouida and Alger, and then the books of exploration and travel. But after that it was Kipling's *Plain Tales from the Hills*, Darwin's *Origin of Species*, Spencer's *Philosophy of Style*, Melville's *Moby-Dick*, and thousands of other works, his reading even extending as far as the theories of Sigmund Freud and Carl Jung, which he was exploring in the last year of his life. In few other writers can we find such a successfully complex intermingling of experience and ideas.

That Jack London became an oyster pirate is not surprising (newspaper articles from that time indicate that hundreds of others were engaged in the same illegal activity each night), and there was nothing particularly remarkable or even romantic about it as far as most of the waterfront workers and hangers-on were concerned. Since California oysters were considered inferior to oysters from the Atlantic Seaboard, seed and yearling oysters from the East Coast were transplanted to the extensive flats at the lower end of the Bay—tidelands that had been grabbed by the Southern Pacific Railroad and leased to oyster growers at rates so prohibitive that within a short time a few large companies had gained control of the entire industry on the coast. This monopoly led to high prices, and soon brought on the oyster pirates. This was not exactly petty crime; every raid on an oyster bed was a felony and the penalty was state imprisonment. But because of general hatred for the Southern Pacific on the part of both the buyers and the police, the oysters could easily be sold at the Oakland docks. It was too good an opportunity for Jack London to pass up, but he did not think of it as simply a way to make some easy money, as most of the other West Oakland thugs did. "I wanted to be where the winds of adventure blew," he writes in *John Barleycorn*. "And the winds of adventure blew the oyster pirate sloops up and down San Francisco Bay, from raided oyster-beds and fights at night on shoal and flat, to markets in the morning against city wharves, where peddlers and saloon keepers came down to buy. . . . And behind it all, behind all of me with youth a-bubble, whispered Romance, Adventure."

This essentially literary concept of his experience later shows up in the two works of fiction that derive from this time, *The Cruise of the Dazzler* (1902) and *Tales of the Fish Patrol* (1905), and of course in *John Barleycorn*, where London claims that he earned the title "Prince of the Oyster Pirates" after he somehow raised three hundred dollars to buy the sloop *Razzle Dazzle* from the fierce French Frank, a notorious oyster pirate in his own right. Even more startling, London tells of how Mamie, French Frank's girl and "Queen of the Oyster Pirates," falls in love with the new owner of the sloop. Throughout his life, London stuck to his story that he borrowed the money to buy the sloop from his childhood nurse, Jennie Prentiss. But like many of the facts London provided about his life, certain questions arise. Three hundred dollars would have been an enormous sum for Mrs. Prentiss to hand over to an adolescent bent upon competing with grown men in what was risky business. The ship could be seized or destroyed in a single night. And why would Mrs. Prentiss want to become London's accomplice in crime? Such questions must be considered in any balanced account of Jack London's life, not to expose the legend so much as to understand that Jack London led a life that was for him inevitably the stuff of books, even if it meant turning what really happened into a lie so that it might, in turn, take on the reality of romance, adventure, and excitement.

A critical commonplace is that Jack London lived a greater story than he wrote.[20] The truth behind most of London's adventures is far different from the stories he wrote about them. Behind *The Cruise of the Dazzler* and *Tales of the Fish Patrol* is a story only partly recounted in the confessional *John Barleycorn*, a story of mad drinking when London would stumble from the saloons so full of "snake poison" that he would fall into the fishing nets on their drying frames and pass out. One time, he nearly drank himself to death on free whiskey provided by politicians at a rally. Another time, he fell into the water while trying to board his sloop at Benicia Pier. London later claimed that he was caught in riptides off Mare Island Light, and that he had a sudden thought of suicide as he was swept away. Four hours later, a Greek fisherman running in for Vallejo pulled him out. At other times he spent as much as $180 a night on drinks, and one of his main ambitions (which he achieved) was to run a tab in Johnny Heinold's account book at the First and Last Chance Saloon.

To this day, much of London's reputation in Oakland is based on sometimes apocryphal accounts of his drinking under the legendary Heinold's tutelage. Heinold, whose bar is still standing, loaned London money several times, became an early advisor, and remained a close friend even after London became famous. And it can be argued that the time London spent in Heinold's saloon had nearly as much to do with his development as a writer as did the adventures he elaborated into stories.

What old-timers at the First and Last Chance most remembered about Jack London, in addition to his prodigious drinking, was his ability to tell a good story at the bar. On this point, Andrew Sinclair writes in his biography of London:

He was not so much a liar as an improver upon the truth, the heir of Mark Twain and Bret Harte and the frontier tradition, which held that the story of a stranger should never deny the pleasure of others for the sake of the facts. So was hard bargaining, treating to drinks, lethal practical jokes, false praise of the fair sex, and an absolute belief that the white man could outfight and outsmart any lesser breed.[21]

It was in the saloons that London first realized the influence a good story could have on his barroom buddies. "We engaged to meet one another in saloons," London recalls in *John Barleycorn*. "We celebrated our good fortune or wept our grief in saloons. We got acquainted in saloons."

Life outside the saloons was another matter. The waterfront along the eastern and northeastern fringes of the Barbary Coast was one of the most dangerous places in the country, so much so that the police usually walked their beats in pairs, each carrying, in addition to a nightstick and revolver, a huge knife a foot or more in length, which they sometimes used to chop off the hands of their assailants. London might easily have been killed in this violent underworld had he not decided to escape it by signing articles as an able seaman on a three-masted sealing schooner bound for the Bonin Islands, the Bering Sea, and Japan. "So I considered my situation and knew that I was getting into a bad way of living," London writes in *John Barleycorn* by way of explaining why he went to sea. He adds that he was getting bored with saloon life, but there may have been more to his decision than a sudden awakening or a lust for adventure. It is entirely possible that London, after four years of running with gangs, oyster-pirating, and petty crime, realized that his luck with the law might be running out.

He had just turned seventeen when the *Sophie Sutherland* (listed in the official register of merchant ships as the *Sophia Sutherland*) passed the Golden Gate. One of twelve sailors in the forecastle, London was challenged to perform a man's work from the start, and his small-boat sailing experience, plus his street-smart ability to defend himself, served him well during "the wild and heavy work off the Siberian coast." In his various accounts of the voyage, however, London's recollections of what happened take on a familiar tone: He won the respect of the crew by winning a fight against a giant Swede; when being chased by the port police in Yokohama, he dived into the harbor and swam a mile to where the *Sophie Sutherland* was anchored; and on the return voyage he took the wheel of the ship during a typhoon and saved both crew and cargo. Concerning the last bit of heroism, it is worth noting that one of Horatio Alger's best-known poems, "John Maynard," tells of a sailor boy who prevents a shipwreck by taking the helm — a story that London essentially retells in "Chris Farrington, Able Seaman" (*The Youth's Companion*, May 1901).

London's description of the Bonin Islands, a small Japanese group in the western Pacific that was used as the rendezvous for the Canadian and American sealing fleets, suggests a further literary connection. On the outward course, and perhaps earlier, London had been reading Melville, whose *Typee*, an account of a sailor's adventures in Polynesia after deserting a whaling ship, comes to mind when reading the description in *John Barleycorn* of the *Sophie Sutherland* sailing in among the reefs to the Bonins: "The scents of strange vegetation blew off the tropic land. Aboriginies, in queer outrigger canoes, and Japanese, in queerer sampans, paddled about the bay and came aboard. It was my first foreign land; I had won to the other side of the world, and I would see all I had read in the books come true. I was wild to get ashore." And, like Melville's hero Tom in *Typee*, London says he wanted to "see beautiful scenery, and strange native villages."

London was to make repeated use of his seven months before the mast — even of the seal-killing itself. "After a good day's killing I have seen our decks covered with hides and bodies, slippery with fat and blood, the scuppers running red," he writes in *The Sea-Wolf* (1904); "masts, ropes, and rails splattered with the sanguinary color; and the men, like butchers plying their trade, naked and red of arm and hand, hard at work with ripping and flensing knives, removing the skins from the pretty sea creatures they had killed." London was a participant in this scene he describes, but in its echoes of the whale-butchering passages in *Moby-Dick* it emphasizes once more how London's response to his adventures was essentially bookish. London was there, doing his part in skinning the seals and salting the hides, but he was consciously seeing his own experiences through the eyes of writers he had read.

This response to his experience led directly to his first published work. When London returned to Oakland, his money was soon gone, and he found a city swept by strikes, lockouts, and riots. The great depression of the 1890s had begun, and wages dropped so low that it took a strong laborer ten hours to earn a dollar—precisely the wage London accepted to wind jute twine in a mill, and precisely the wage he later accepted to shovel coal at the power plant of the Oakland, San Leandro, and Haywards Electric Railway. But while he was sweating as a "work-beast," he produced "Story of a Typhoon off the Coast of Japan," which won twenty-five dollars in a contest for young writers that was sponsored by the San Francisco *Morning Call*. His mother had mentioned the contest to him, and, knowing London's reputation as a storyteller, had encouraged him to enter it.

This narrative, written when London was still seventeen, is startlingly good, full of striking imagery and hard-driving sentences. "The wild antics of the schooner were sickening as she forged along," London writes.

She would almost stop as though climbing a mountain, then rapidly rolling to right and left as she gained the summit of a huge sea, she steadied herself and paused for a moment as though affrighted at the yawning precipice before her. Like an avalanche she shot forward and down as the sea astern struck her with the force of a thousand battering rams, burying her bow to the catheads in the milky foam at the bottom that came on deck in all directions—forward, astern, to right and to left, through the hawse pipes and over the rail.[22]

That London could write so well at that point in his life startled even his daughter when she read it many years later. "Jack's production of this prize-winning narrative at this time is a matter of no little accomplishment," she comments. "It is well, even skillfully written, with a sureness that seems to betoken practice and experience. . . . There is no telling. One searches in vain either for earlier writings or intimations that an impulse to express himself in this way had been manifested before."[23] But the source is easily enough found. London had read stories of a similar kind in Dana's *Two Years Before the Mast*, in Captain Cook's *Voyages*, and in Melville. He had heard stories of a somewhat different sort in the saloons. And he had his own typhoon experience to tell when he walked into the First and Last Chance upon his return from Japan. When he sat down to write it, he told it in the best saloon fashion, never denying the pleasure of others for the sake of the facts.

London tried to follow up his first success by submitting other pieces to the *Morning Call*, but once the contest was over the editor said he had no more use for London's sea stories. London apparently sent some of them to other publications, but had no success. He was tempted to return to the waterfront, and he could have gone to sea again, but for a while decided to try something else. Desperate, drinking once again, sick of contemplating life as a work-beast in a jute mill or a power plant, London did what thousands of others were doing at the time — he took to the road in the second of the great escapes that gave structure to his life.

London was not alone in his desperation. It has been estimated that three million men and women were unemployed in the United States in 1894, and armies of homeless tramps were terrorizing communities across the country. But one man, as has so often happened in a nation of naive philosophers and inventors, had a solution. Jacob Coxey, a prominent citizen of Massillon, Ohio (birthplace, coincidentally of London's mother), planned to lead a march of twenty thousand unemployed to Washington, where a petition would be presented to Congress insisting that something be done to relieve the moral distress.

Coxey believed that the ultimate solution was to convert the United States into a true Christian commonwealth. His assistant, Carl Browne, a Theosophist from Calistoga, California, liked to display a large portrait he had painted of Jesus Christ bearing the inscription "PEACE ON EARTH Good Will toward Men! He hath risen!!! BUT DEATH TO INTEREST ON BONDS!!!" Christ's features on the portrait suspiciously resembled those of the painter himself (and Browne at times claimed that he was Christ's reincarnated soul). The movement of Coxey and Browne pretty much broke down before it reached Washington, and Coxey was ingloriously arrested for walking on the Capital lawns, but several "Coxey Bills" were introduced into the Senate by sympathetic Populists. One such measure was to allow any legitimate governing body to issue non-interest-bearing bonds to finance public improvements and to provide work for the unemployed. Another bill called for the printing of half a billion dollars to employ the jobless in improving the county-road system of the United States. Coxey, who

lived until 1951, when he turned ninety-seven (and
who was an agitator down to the end), was an early
advocate of what would later be termed Keynesian economics. He believed that the best weapon against economic depression is government spending on public
works, and his ideas are reworked by London in the
principles of the Oligarchy's rule in *The Iron Heel* (1908).

Coxey's army had a West Coast contingent, the
Industrial Army, recruited by a thirty-two-year-old
printer named Charles Kelly. At its peak, this army
numbered nearly two thousand men, among them Jack
London, who joined the Reno detachment on April 17.
Traveling by train (sometimes commandeering empty
boxcars and refrigerator cars), by wagon, and by foot,
and panhandling for food along the way, the army
made its way eastward, often fed by terrified townsfolk
who simply wanted it to move on. Many members of
the army were hoboes who had enlisted because of the
free benefits they hoped to receive. But many others
were genuinely committed political radicals who saw
the march as the first step toward the abolition of the
class system, the opposition of capital, and the establishment of a socialist order. "At night as they ate supper and prepared for bed, or sat about the campfire on
fine nights, the men engaged in endless discussions,"
Joan London writes of her father. "Everyone had something to say, and every variety of panacea, from single
tax to astrology, was offered to solve the depression.
There were numbers of trade unionists in the army,
many chronically unemployed hoboes, a sprinkling of
Socialists and even a few declassed members of the
petty bourgeoisie. Jack listened to them all."[24]

This would not have been the first time London
had heard the doctrines of socialism expounded, but it
is clear that he was impressed by the logic of the socialists, which was reinforced by his experiences on the
road. In his essay "How I Became a Socialist" (1905)

London explains: "I found myself looking upon life from a new and totally different angle. I had dropped down from the proletariat into what sociologists love to call the 'submerged tenth,' and I was startled to discover the way in which that submerged tenth was recruited." And earlier in the same essay he emphasizes, "It is quite fair to say that I became a Socialist in fashion somewhat similar to the way in which the Teutonic pagans became Christians — it was hammered into me." Along with it, as he watched the fights, the scrounging for food, and the drinking bouts, he solidified his thinking on another idea that was to run through his writing and work its way into the radical political consciousness awakened in him by socialism: the doctrine of the survival of the fittest.

This doctrine was to be brutally demonstrated for London again and again, but most dramatically after he dropped out of Kelly's Army at Hannibal, Missouri, and traveled north and east to Ottawa and Montreal, New York, Boston, Pittsburgh, Baltimore (his exact itinerary is uncertain), and finally to Niagara Falls, where he was arrested for vagrancy and sentenced to thirty days in the Erie County Penitentiary.

This was one of the most emotionally devastating months in London's life. He was marched with a small chain gang of other hoboes to the railroad station and transported to the prison. The men were taken into the barber shop and ordered to strip, bathe, and lather themselves to be shaved bald. This is an experience London later wrote about in *The Road* (1907), but he was never able to deal directly with what he went through in having to submit to the friendship of an older inmate — "cottoning" to his "meat," in jail slang — to survive. After two days, thanks to the influence of his pal, London was made a "hallman," taking bread and water to the other prisoners evenings and mornings, thus gaining access to extra rations, which he was able

to trade for chewing tobacco and other privileges — but
at what price he was never able to say.

London did not write about sexual matters very
directly, yet in the prison scenes of *The Road* there is an
undertone of revulsion indicating that London's tough-
guy, survival-of-the-fittest account of his time in jail
does not say it all. London's month at the Erie Penitentiary shook the romance of the hobo life out of him. He
was forced to endure unnamed degradations in a place
he described as "a common stews, filled with the ruck
and the filth, the scum and dregs, of society — hereditary inefficients, degenerates, wrecks, lunatics, addled
intelligences, epileptics, monsters, weaklings, in short,
a very nightmare of humanity." The older inmate who
had gotten London the run of the prison also expected
him to continue on as his partner in petty crime when
they were released, but London ditched him in a tavern
on the day of their release and a few minutes later was
on board a freight headed, however indirectly, back to
California, some tough lessons learned.

While on the road, London had started the practice of keeping a diary, and his apparent resolve to
become a writer was tied in with his enrollment, close
to his nineteenth birthday, at Oakland High School.
His decision to become a student was strongly supported by his mother and his stepsister Eliza. His mother
fixed up a combination bedroom and den in the small
house at 1639 Twenty-second Avenue in East Oakland,
and Eliza provided him with a study table and a bicycle — as well as with a set of false upper teeth (his own
were the victims of decay and "accidents" sustained on
his travels). Within a few weeks after starting school,
London had his two-part article on the "Bonin Islands"
published in *The High School Aegis* (January 18 and February 1, 1895). During the year, he submitted eight more
articles and short stories — all of which were published
— at the same time throwing himself into his studies.

But high school soon lost much of its appeal for London, whose experiences and growing political radicalism, as well as his workingman's clothing and tendency to lapse into the rough expressions of his sailor and hobo days, set him apart from most of the other students. As he grew more impatient with his studies and teachers, and as he increasingly came to believe that he could learn faster on his own, his visits to the Oakland Public Library became more frequent. It was at the library that he met a young man named Fred Jacobs, who was working in the reference room to earn enough money to pay for a year at the University Academy, a "cramming joint" in Alameda where he hoped he could prepare to take the entrance examination for the University of California. Jacobs introduced some of his friends to London, including Ted and Mabel Applegarth, and Bess Maddern, who was to become London's first wife.

London was soon drawn into a world that seemed to him to be all taste and refinement, although it was merely one of respectability. The Applegarths' father was a successful mining engineer, and their mother believed in raising the children according to British middle-class standards (the family had come to Oakland from England). This involved music and table manners and a variety of old-fashioned courtesies with which London had virtually no acquaintance. It also involved British nineteenth-century poets, bicycle trips, picnic suppers, and chess (which Jack learned from Ted). For a time, however, all of this was dimmed by the presence of Mabel Applegarth herself. She was beautiful in a slender, frail way, and London's attempts to eliminate all roughness from his speech, and his efforts at other forms of self- improvement (more stylish clothing, a developing interest in opera, and a sudden desire to become "cultured"), can all be attributed to his infatuation with her. His impatient rage for suc-

cess, which soon overwhelmed him and led to his quitting high school in favor of the cramming academy and
eventual admission to the University of California, can
also be partly attributed to her influence.

For a time, London was studying nineteen hours a
day, getting help from Mabel in English, Fred Jacobs in
chemistry and physics, and Bess Maddern in advanced
mathematics. On August 10, 1896, London pedaled
his bicycle to Berkeley and began the three-day entrance exams. He had studied so long and so hard that
he was suffering from nervous twitches and somewhat
curious intellectual delusions (at one point he believed
he had discovered the formula for squaring a circle),
but he passed with little trouble and was cleared to
enter the university in the fall. He celebrated by borrowing a boat, sailing to Benicia, and drinking with his
old friends. But it was the world of the Applegarths that
held the greatest attraction for him, and he believed
that a university education would gain him full admission to that world.

London lasted little more than a term at the University of California. He signed up for two history
courses (Europe during the Middle Ages and political
history of the nineteenth century) and three English
courses (composition, history of English literature, and
composition based on nineteenth-century science writers Darwin, Huxley, Spencer, and Tyndall). When
London left the university on February 4, 1897, with
an Honorable Dismissal, he had earned an A and a B
in the history courses but had incompletes in the English courses. London never fully explained why he left
Berkeley so soon, but the likeliest explanation for his
short academic career is that the university simply was
not what he thought it would be.[25] Older than most of
the other students, certainly more experienced in the
ways of the world, never a very patient scholar, and
filled with gigantic plans for himself, London later ex-

pressed his collegiate discontentment in an essay, "Phenomena of Literary Evolution" (*The Bookman*, October 1900): "The student refuses to sit under a professor who lectures after the fashion of the kindergarten. It drives him mad to have all things and the most obvious things explained at length. He would as soon sit down and read Defoe in words of one syllable or do sums in arithmetic on his fingers." Besides, he had become interested in lectures of a different kind.

On his way to and from the Oakland Public Library, London would often stop to listen to the socialist orators who held forth in City Hall Park, and soon he was attending the Socialist Labor Party's Sunday-evening lectures and outdoor meetings. In April 1896, London formally joined the party, began signing some of his letters "Yours for the Revolution," wrote rabid letters to newspapers, and soon was being referred to by the same newspapers as the "boy socialist." Even before he received the small red booklet that contained his membership card, London had achieved some notoriety for his views, and the San Francisco *Chronicle* of February 16, 1896, printed a concise description of both London and his ideas as he held forth nightly to the crowds that thronged City Hall Park: "The young man is a pleasant speaker, more earnest than eloquent, and while he is a broad socialist in every way, he is not an Anarchist. He says on the subject, when asked for a definition of socialism, 'It is an all-embracing term — communists, nationalists, collectionists, idealists, utopians, altrurians, are all socialists, but it cannot be said that socialism is any of these — it is all.'"

Socialism soon became for London what spiritualism was to his mother and astrology was to his father: a bundle of wildly speculative beliefs and theories that seemed to have universal application. After he read one of the basic books in the socialist movement, Herbert Spencer's *First Principles* (1862), he believed that Spen-

cer had organized all knowledge for him, had provided
him with a kind of cosmogonic gunnysack for all philosophy. Famous for coining the slogan "survival of the
fittest," Spencer attempted, through his "Synthetic Philosophy," to summarize all knowledge under one focal
theme: an optimistic interpretation of evolution, asserting that evolution is synonymous with progress in life,
mind, morality, society, and the cosmos, and that
through inevitable social change evil and immorality
must disappear. Such a philosophy had automatic appeal to a socialist such as London was becoming. And
London's devotion to Spencer points to something else.
As widely read as London was, even as a young man, he
was to remain something of a believer in various "systems"
throughout his life that would offer him a secure intellectual framework. "Mr. Spencer's contribution to the
world's knowledge is so great that we cannot appreciate
it," London once stated. "We lack perspective. Only
future centuries may measure his work for what it is;
and when a thousand generations of fiction writers
have been laid away, one upon another, and forgotten,
Spencer will be even better known than in this day."[2b]

London's simultaneous courting of Mabel Applegarth along with his growing involvement in the socialist movement are, of course, contradictory. On the one
side was genteel respectability, on the other radicalism
and bloody visions of class war in the streets. This was
a contradiction London was never to resolve, and he
has been attacked again and again for using his scandalous reputation as a socialist to further increase the
sales of his books and to provide him with the money
that would make him someday far wealthier than the
Applegarths would perhaps have considered decent.
But the probable truth is that London found his fellow
socialists and their sometimes outrageous behavior far
more exciting than the "pale gold flower upon a slender
stem" — as he describes Mabel's fictional counterpart in
Martin Eden.

How different his interests and changing attitudes were from those of the Applegarths can be gauged in an incident that occurred shortly after London dropped out of college. On February 12, 1897, he stepped up on a soapbox as the main speaker on a Lincoln's Birthday meeting organized to protest Oakland Ordinance No. 1676, which forbade speaking at any public meeting on any public street without the written permission of the mayor. London was arrested and hauled off to jail, demanded a jury trial (held on February 18), spoke in his own defense, and won his acquittal, with the result that the Oakland Socialists tried to capitalize on his fame by nominating him for the Oakland School Board.

After his encounter with the law was behind him (the judge released him with a caution), London faced a more immediate problem than a hopeless campaign for a school board post: how to make a living. For a few weeks he tried to get a writing career started, working on a borrowed typewriter that would punch out only capital letters. He attempted stories, ponderous essays (after the manner of Spencer), and even a blank-verse tragedy. But he got nowhere, and soon he was selling his secondhand schoolbooks, borrowing money from his sister and Johnny Heinold, and eventually reaching the point where he was forced to take a job sorting, washing, and ironing laundry at Belmont Academy, a military school south of San Francisco on the peninsula. He and his partner got thirty dollars a month plus room and board, working six days a week, spending Sundays too exhausted to even begin reading the trunkful of books he had brought along. When the academy closed for the summer and London could pack his things and go back to Oakland, he did not know what he could do. He feared he would become a work-beast again for good.

Instead, he embarked on his greatest adventure: his fantastically embellished trip to the Klondike gold fields, a trip that would contribute greatly to the Jack London legend and, more important, provide him with the material for his greatest work. London, like thousands of others, got caught up in the madness that followed the docking of the S.S. *Excelsior* on July 14, 1897, in San Francisco and the announcement by a few unkempt men that they had struck it rich in the region surrounding the Klondike River in the west Yukon Territory of Canada. To London's surprise, his sister Eliza's elderly husband, James Shepard, had come down with gold-rush fever himself, convinced his wife to mortgage their house and shares in a small business in order to put together a grubstake, and offered to take London along as his partner. On July 25, 1897, the two men sailed on the S.S. *Umatilla*, each with enough supplies to last a year. London's own outfit weighed nearly two thousand pounds.

One of London's favorite sayings was that "It was in the Klondike that I found myself. There nobody talks. Everybody thinks. You get your perspective. I got mine."[27] True enough, as London's writing certainly attests; but simply getting to the Klondike presented a challenge that forced all those who attempted it to confront their deepest selves. James Shepard was not to be one of those. When he saw the difficulty of transporting supplies over the Chilkoot Pass, he simply gave up, left his share of the equipment and Jack's share of the money they had brought along, and took the next steamship home. London did not push on alone, however; during the voyage north he had entered into a travel agreement with three other men, and together they got their supplies over the pass and across lakes Linderman and Bennett in a boat they built out of boards whipsawed from fresh-cut trees. They went down Lake Marsh and the Sixtymile River, through Box Canyon and White

Horse Rapids, over Lake LeBarge (made famous by Robert Service's poem "The Cremation of Sam McGee"), and ultimately to the Yukon River and Split-Up Island (also called Upper Island), eighty miles from Dawson, where they intended to spend the winter in an old cabin that had been abandoned by the Bering Sea fur traders of the Alaska Commercial Company.

London was always eager to take credit for his heroics on the journey, and it was this as much as anything that most contributed to London's folk-hero stature. The trip was tough and dangerous, and anyone who survived the ordeal long enough to get to Dawson deserved the fullest credit. The final climb to Chilkoot Pass, for instance, was about three-quarters of a mile in length and in places had an average slope of about forty-five degrees. London claimed that he carried packs weighing as much as 150 pounds as his party hauled their supplies up and over the pass and down to Lake Linderman. Once on the water, London boasted of his sailing experience and took credit for steering dozens of boats through White Horse Rapids, charging twenty-five dollars each and earning three thousand dollars while a thousand people watched and cheered. The Klondike was a place where tall tales abounded.

London did apply for placer-mining claim Number 54 on the left fork ascending Henderson Creek, not far from Split-Up Island, and swore before the Gold Commissioner in Dawson that he had discovered a deposit. He did little mining, although modern gold dredges have subsequently proved that London's claim was indeed a rich one. Instead, he spent about six weeks in Dawson after he filed the claim, hanging around the saloons — the Moosehorn, the Eldorado, the Elkhorn, and others — that served the ramshackle city of five thousand mostly lonely and disappointed men, and a small but thriving population of dance-hall girls and prostitutes. One of the few men who had genuine recollections of London in the Klondike recalled meeting him in a Dawson bar during the fall of 1897 and remembered that he "was surely prospecting, but it was at bars that he sought his material. I believe that he had staked a claim, and it is probable that his hatred of capitalism did not extend to acquiring wealth for himself, but I never saw him working one, never met him on the trail, and do not remember ever having seen him except in some Dawson bar."[28]

London returned to Split-Up Island for the winter and spent his time reading, arguing, playing cards, eating the three "B's" of the sourdough's rations (biscuits, beans, and bacon), and lying in his bunk for hours at a time. In 1969 an expedition led by Russ Kingman, author of *A Pictorial Life of Jack London*, the actor and London enthusiast Eddie Albert, and several Oakland city officials traveled to the island and found London's signature scrawled high on the back wall of a cabin near Henderson Creek. The date was January 27, 1898, and after his name London had added "Author/Miner."[29] But by May, London was in rough shape. Like many other Klondike adventurers, he had developed scurvy from a lack of fresh vegetables and fruit. When he got to Dawson after the ice breakup, he had trouble walking, was covered with sores, and his teeth were loose in their sockets. After receiving some rudimentary treatment at the Catholic hospital, London floated fifteen hundred miles down the Yukon with two other men in a skiff to the harbor at St. Michael's on the Bering Sea. It is uncertain how he got back to Oakland, but it is likely that London took a job as stoker on a boat to British Columbia, made his way to Seattle, and then rode freight trains home. He arrived sick, exhausted, and broke, but determined to begin his real career.

Actually, it had already begun, but in a peculiar way. While he was struggling over the Chilkoot Pass in

September 1897, *The Owl Magazine* published "Two
Gold Bricks," a story reflecting his early experiences
with spiritualism. But apparently London never saw
the magazine or even knew that the story had appeared. Its existence does indicate, however, that London's conception of himself as a writer predates his
Klondike adventures and that the trip north may have
been more of a deliberate search for material than has
been presumed. At least some of this material went
into the diary London 'began keeping on the trip
down the Yukon to St. Michael's, and when he returned to Oakland he pawned his bicycle, his watch,
and even his raincoat so that he could write. His stepfather had died while he was gone, and, even though his
mother was struggling to keep up with the rent, she
encouraged her son to pursue his ambition. He sent an
article entitled "From Dawson to the Sea" to the San
Francisco *Bulletin* and promptly got it back, the editor
writing that so much had been written about the gold
rush that there was no point in publishing another personal sketch. London sat down and wrote a twenty-
thousand-word serial for *Youth's Companion* in seven days.
Not only was it rejected, but the magazine editor ad-
vised London to forget about a writing career. London
himself had his doubts, evidenced in his taking an examination for a job as mail carrier at the Oakland Post
Office on October 1.

The assumption has long been that this was a time
of blind and feverish writing for London, with rejection
slips piling up in his room and London despairing of
ever succeeding. This is a notion London himself encouraged. In an essay written for *Editor* magazine in
1903, London lamented that all of his manuscripts
came back and that

The process seemed like the working of a soulless machine. I
dropped the manuscript into the mail box. After the lapse of

a certain approximate length of time, the manuscript was brought back to me by the postman. Accompanying it was a stereotyped rejection slip. A part of the machine, some cunning arrangement of cogs and cranks at the other end (it could not have been a living, breathing man with blood in his veins) had transferred the manuscript to another envelope, taken the stamps from the inside and pasted them on the outside, and added the rejection slip.[30]

In fact, London's success was relatively sudden once he settled down at his desk following his return from the Klondike. Within six months the *Overland Monthly* had accepted the first of his Northland stories, "To the Man on Trail," and in February of 1899 *The Black Cat* paid him forty dollars for his horror story "A Thousand Deaths." In the middle of the same month, James Howard Bridge, the editor of the *Overland Monthly* (having already published "The White Silence"), offered a contract for six more stories, promising that although the pay would be only seven dollars and fifty cents each, the stories would be given prominent display in the magazine and were bound to attract the attention of reviewers, critics, and (most important) higher-paying outlets.

London could not have found a better first market. With its editorial headquarters in San Francisco, the *Overland Monthly*, founded in 1868, had as its main purpose the promotion of Western literature, and the editors had established a policy of helping young Western writers. Charles Warren Stoddard, Bret Harte, and Ina Coolbrith — known as the "Golden Gate Trinity" — had written for the magazine, and London's early work soon earned him an identity that only the *Overland Monthly* could provide. As a consequence, his work was taken seriously from the start. George Hamlin Fitch, literary critic of the San Francisco *Chronicle*, said in his review of the February number of the *Overland*, "I would rather have written 'The White Silence' than anything that has appeared in fiction in the last ten years."[31] London published his work in a variety of magazines in 1899, ranging from the *Illustrated Buffalo Express* to the *American Agriculturalist* to *New England Homestead*, but it was the *Overland Monthly* that first gained him the recognition that led to an acceptance check of $120 from the *Atlantic Monthly* on October 30, 1899, for "An Odyssey of the North," which was published in the first issue of 1900. After this acceptance, London sent a collection of his stories to Houghton Mifflin & Co. of Boston. The result was *The Son of the Wolf*, London's first book of stories, published in April 1900, which was so well received that in a little over a year and a half after he had showed up broke in Oakland, he was being touted as not only the Bret Harte of the Yukon but the Kipling of the Klondike.

London's prompt development was the consequence of a thoroughly professional attitude. Not only did he set himself to writing a quota of at least a thousand words a day, Sundays and holidays included (a practice he was to hold to the rest of his life), but he also studied his market like a broker. He dissected short stories in current magazines; he devised a system of vocabulary building; he looked into such handbooks as Charles R. Barrett's *Short Story Writing: A Practical Treatise on the Art of the Short Story*, which appeared in 1898; and he set up a bookkeeping system that enabled him to know where his manuscripts were, which magazines had rejected them, and even how much he had spent on stamps to send out a given story.

London, of course, appeared on the literary scene at a time when there was an enormous market for short stories, particularly adventure stories of the sort that were to earn him his first fame. Improvements in photoengraving and new techniques in the manufacture of paper lowered printing costs and made possible popular magazines such as *Munsey's, McClure's,* and *Cosmopoli-*

tan that could be sold for ten cents a copy (the older magazines, like *Harper's* and *The Century*, typically sold for twenty-five cents). The new magazines could achieve huge circulations by appealing to an audience that, in its tastes for the sensational, offered publishers the possibilities of enormous profits. London understood this market and its audience well. His experiences, his reading, and his thorough professionalism from the start made a perfect blend at a time when the best-paying magazines wanted to please a public hungry for stories of strength, virility, and adventure. London sought to meet this need, and he knew just what he was doing. "His work was realism," he writes of his alter ego in *Martin Eden*, "though he endeavored to fuse it with the fancies and beauties of imagination. What he sought was an impassioned realism, shot through with human aspiration and faith. What he wanted was life as it was, with all its spirit-groping and soul-reaching left in."

In addition to appearing on the literary scene at the height of what has since come to be termed the golden age of the magazine, London was fortunate in that his stories, with their emphasis on toughness and savagery displayed against the setting of the wilderness of the far north or the raging Pacific, coincided with an era now known as the "Strenuous Age" — the Teddy Roosevelt years, when there was the widespread notion that, because of the disappearance of the frontier and the "pollution" of the American spirit through excessive immigration, the country had "gone soft" and needed to shape up by regaining the virtues of the pioneer past.

This idea received dramatic statement after 1893 in the essays of the Wisconsin historian Frederick Jackson Turner. Turner's most famous essay is the paper he delivered at the annual convention of the American Historical Society in 1893. He argued that, with the disappearance of the frontier, the first period in American history had ended, and with it had gone the reinvigorating potential of the fresh start so crucial to American social development. But the article that was most widely discussed during the decade appeared in the *Atlantic Monthly* for September 1896. Turner began by arguing that the frontier not only made the American different from the European; it made him better. "Out of his wilderness experience," Turner wrote, "out of the freedom of his opportunities, he fashioned a formula for social regeneration — the freedom of the individual to seek his own."[12] Turner finished by linking the idea of the wild with sacred American virtues and stressing the importance of retaining the influence of the wilderness in modern civilization.

These attitudes were anticipated by Teddy Roosevelt himself in his 1889 book, *The Winning of the West*, in which he wrote, "Under the hard conditions of life in the wilderness" those who came to the New World were transformed, revitalized, "in dress, in customs, and mode of life."[13] The result was a "wilderness cult" that had its impact on the conservation movement and led to the founding of such outdoor magazines as *Field and Stream* in 1895, the establishment of the Boy Scouts of America (the first edition of the Scouts' *Handbook* in 1910 encouraged the boys of America to counter "degeneracy" by demonstrating the wholesome values of "Outdoor Life"), and the organization of the Sierra Club, the Boone and Crockett Club, and hundreds of rod-and-gun clubs across the country. It also had an impact on the reading tastes of Americans. What was called "Natural History" became an important genre, and such books as John Muir's *The Mountains of California* (1893) quickly sold out. John Burroughs, with his articles and books on birds and animals, was one of the most famous public figures of the time. And, of course, *The Call of the Wild* (1903) firmly established the reputation of Jack London as a writer who fully understood the redemptive virtues of the primitive environment, because he had been there and it had made him strong.

The reader's report to Houghton Mifflin on *The Son of the Wolf* illustrates how startlingly well London's work meshed with the ideals of the Strenuous Age and the concurrent wilderness mania. "He uses the current slang of the mining camps a little too freely, but his style has freshness, vigor and strength," the reader wrote in advocating acceptance of the collection. "He draws a vivid picture of the terrors of cold, darkness, and starvation, the pleasures of human companionship in adverse circumstances, and the sterling qualities which the rough battle with nature brings out. The reader is convinced that the author has lived the life himself."[34]

London was living another kind of life as well. With friends he had met at Socialist Labor Party debates, he was building a reputation as a platform speaker and a socialist intellectual. In July 1899, when *Cosmopolitan* announced a two-hundred-dollar prize for the best article on "Loss by Lack of Co-operation," London put together what he had learned through socialist meetings, lectures, and debates and won the contest with an essay entitled, "What Communities Lose by the Competitive System"—later joking to his comrades, "I guess I'm the only man in America who is making money out of socialism."[35]

So animated was he in discussions, so voluble was he in advocating overthrow of the existing order and the redefinition of sexual freedom and marriage, that some of his friends thought that he had suffered a stroke or some kind of breakdown when he announced early in April, 1900, that he intended to marry Bess Maddern. This seemed especially disconcerting since he had been spending much of his time with Anna Strunsky, whom he had met at a lecture in the old Turk Street Temple in San Francisco the previous fall.

Two years younger than London, and thought of

as a great beauty with her dark eyes, high cheekbones, and lustrous black hair, Anna was from a Russian-Jewish family that took pride in its connections with Emma Goldman and other radicals. Anna herself had been called the "girl socialist" of San Francisco. Soon London was addressing her as "Dear, dear You" in his letters, and they were to collaborate in a curious dialogue assessing the merits of scientific versus romantic love that would result in *The Kempton-Wace Letters* (1903). London was immediately drawn to Anna, yet he had already developed an image of himself as a hard man, one who believed he had to live by the rule of cold logic. "He systematized his life," Anna wrote in trying to explain what had happened between them. "Such colossal energy, and yet he could not trust himself! He lived by rule. Law, Order, and Restraint was the creed of this vital, passionate youth."[36] And like many of his other friends, Anna was suspicious of London's somewhat desperate rationalizations of his own uncontrollable desires, fierce appetites, and inconsistencies.

That London would turn from Anna Strunsky to Bess Maddern seems at first to be another example of the contradictory impulses that show up again and again in his life. Yet he had known Bess since at least 1895 and had spent afternoons bicycling with her to picnics or evenings going to the opera. She had tutored him in mathematics when he was cramming for admission to the university, and she had a handsome figure and steady nature that were appealing to London in the midst of his thousand-word-a-day regimen, his political activities, and the long nights of reading as he struggled to get what he called his "scientific basis."

The daughter of a plumber, Bess Maddern was athletic and vigorous, with blue-black hair and hazel eyes. She had gone to business school, had aspirations for the university, and could possibly have had a career as an actress. She was the cousin of Minnie Maddern Fiske, well known on the New York stage, who had

asked that Bess be placed under her care and training;
but Bess's parents refused to allow it (as would London
himself when the same request was made concerning
his daughter, Joan). Bess had the talents that come out
of a combination of self-control and an essentially good
nature, and as impulsive as London's marriage proposal may have been, he saw her as a woman not only
strong enough to produce "seven Saxon sons" but also
good enough to make a better man out of him. "I shall
be steadied, and can be able to devote more time to my
work," he wrote to Mrs. Ninetta Eames, wife of the
business manager of the *Overland Monthly*. "One only has
one life, after all, and why not live it? Besides, my heart
is large, and I shall be a cleaner, wholesomer man
because of a restraint being laid upon me instead of
being free to drift wheresoever I listed. I am sure you
will understand."[37] On April 7, 1900, London married
Bess in the Madderns' home. A little over three years
later they would be separated; in 1905 they would be
divorced.

In explaining his marriage, London claimed that
he told Bess at the outset he did not love her and that he
had adopted a theory of marriage that precluded romantic love. Much of the impulsiveness in London's
personality can be attributed to his willingness to put
every action, every decision to the test of an idea or
theory — sometimes with pathetic results. London's attitude toward marriage comes out clearly enough in the
sentiments of Herbert Wace, his mouthpiece in *The
Kempton-Wace Letters*. Probably as early as 1900 London
had asked Anna Strunsky to collaborate with him on a
book in which he would play the role of a young economics professor who believed in logic and evolution,
and she would be an older friend, Dane Kempton, who
believed in romantic idealism. It was to be a dangerous
arrangement, and Anna Strunsky's name was mentioned at one point in London's divorce proceedings.

But what was more damaging to the marriage itself was the doctrine London had Wace espouse. "No, I am not in love," Wace says as he contemplates marriage. "I am very thankful that I am not. . . . I am arranging my life so that I can get the most out of it, while the one thing to disorder it, worse than flood and fire and the public enemy, is love." To Wace, "Love is a disorder of mind and body." It is simply "a means for the perpetuation and development of the human type" and can be improved and controlled by the intellect.

London's posture through much of the book is pathologically clinical, and Anna Strunsky as Dane Kempton moves toward the same reaction most readers would have: that London/Wace is "in the toils of an idea, the idea of selection, and that he exploits it like a drudge"—somewhat after the manner of London's mentor, Herbert Spencer, who once coldly drew up opposing lists of the advantages and disadvantages of marriage, and decided to remain a bachelor. Given such attitudes, it is surprising that London's marriage lasted as long as it did. And when it was over, he had to admit his essential mistake. A few weeks after his separation, he told a friend, "It's all right for a man sometimes to marry philosophically, but remember, it's damned hard on the woman."[38]

Joan London's remark about her father, that "He was to study and master much in his life, but knowledge of women would always elude him,"[39] certainly applies to this crucial period of his life that he was later to term "the long sickness." He was steadily improving his income thanks in part to the 125-dollar monthly advance against future work offered by S.S. McClure in 1900, which was followed by a 150-dollar-a-month offer by George Brett of Macmillan in 1902. London was eventually able to move Bess and his young family (Joan was born in 1901, Becky in 1902) into a large bungalow overlooking San Francisco Bay in the Pied-

mont Hills above Oakland. Nonetheless, he persisted
in his pursuit of Anna Strunsky, and in 1902 actually
proposed marriage to her, suggesting that they escape
together to Australia and New Zealand. At the same
time, he was becoming involved with Charmian Kittredge, the niece of Ninetta Eames. He was also spending more and more time with the growing circle of
friends who attended the famous Wednesday-evening
gatherings at his house for drinks, discussion, and
horseplay — gatherings that became increasingly disturbing to London's wife. But it was Charmian she
should have worried about the most.

Five years older than London, Charmian Kittredge worked as a secretary, had managed to save
enough for a trip to Europe, and generally affected the
style of the "new woman," which mainly meant that she
smoked, wore what then passed for casual clothing, and
could talk freely and frankly about censored books and
post-Victorian sexual practices. She soon took on the
image of the ideal "Mate-Woman" London describes in
The Kempton-Wace Letters: "wonderful and unmoral and
filled with life to the brim." Perhaps more significantly,
she also seemed to be the embodiment of Frona Welse,
the astonishing heroine of London's first "adult" novel,
A Daughter of the Snows (1902). Frona, "fair and flaxen
haired, typically Saxon," arrives in the Yukon full of
feminine charm and bulging biceps, able to recite entire passages from Spencer, and capable of driving a
dog sled twenty miles at seventy-below. Charmian became for London what Anna refused to be and what
Bess could never be: the dream girl of his first real, and
in many ways least convincing, novel.

Jack London married Charmian Kittredge on November 19, 1905, in Chicago. She stayed with him until his
death in 1916. She was often criticized by his friends,

but she typed his manuscripts, read proofs (her editing
of London's work may, at times, have been extensive),
endured sometimes humiliating hardship while on
many of their travels, and down to the end continued to
address her husband as "Mate-Man."

London's first marriage, at any rate, did not make
him "a cleaner, wholesomer man" for long. Memoirs by
friends and contemporaries attest that he often reacted
to marital spats by taking off for the Barbary Coast and
a night of drinking whiskey and whoring (a charge in
the divorce petition was that London had contracted
gonorrhea). One of his frequent companions on such
expeditions was George Sterling, minor poet and a dis-
ciple of Ambrose Bierce, one of California's leading
literary figures, now known mostly for his grumpy collection of satiric epigrams, *The Devil's Dictionary*, and
such short stories as the much-anthologized "An Occurrence at Owl Creek Bridge." The friendship between
London and Sterling soon involved more than nights
on the town.

London called Sterling — remembered by many as
looking like the "ideal poet," and still a legendary figure
around San Francisco — "Greek." Sterling repaid the
compliment by calling London "Wolf" and beginning
letters with "My Darling Wolf." The two remained close
for years, each seeming to remedy a defect in the other.
Sterling at least partially succeeded in making something of a hedonist out of London, introducing him to
gourmet food and making him more fastidious; London, in turn, introduced Sterling to a low-life physical
world of women, sport, and rough pleasures. Both were
men of many quirks. Sterling always carried a vial of
cyanide of potassium in the lower left-hand pocket of
his vest, claiming that when the time was right he
would take it — which he did, committing suicide in
1926. Sterling also loved to be photographed in the

nude, and London himself took some of the pictures. Many writers have remarked on the sexuality in the relationship, but both men would have furiously resented any inference of latent homosexuality. London's affection for Sterling, by most accounts, was a shared love of the games, the discussions, and the general hijinks of what both of them referred to as the "Crowd" — Jim Whitaker, Frank Strawn-Hamilton, Anna Strunsky, Charmian Kittredge, and Sterling himself — the friends who offered London the fun and companionship he thought had been denied him in his boyhood. With them   London went on picnics, flew kites, demonstrated his repertoire of magic tricks, and played practical jokes.

But the most direct explanation of London's close friendship with Sterling is that the poet had provided him with support and understanding during "the long sickness" and had helped him move away from the cold rationalism he had used in justifying his marriage to Bess. Years of hard work combined with heavy drinking had left London feeling isolated and miserable, fearing that his nerve would fail him in mid-career. But at the end, London believed that his friendship with Sterling and his marriage to Charmian had saved him, and that both had helped him regain his basic cheerfulness by encouraging him not to pursue ideas blindly in the way that led to the foolishness of his first marriage. "I had read too much positive science and lived too much positive life," London admits in *John Barleycorn*.

But while he had learned the danger of embracing hard ideas too coldly, he nonetheless devoted himself more and more to what he saw as the great cause of his time. "There was still one fight left in me," London could proclaim in *John Barleycorn*, "and here was the thing for which to fight. I threw all precaution to the winds, threw myself into the fight for socialism, laughed at the editors and publishers who warned me and was brutally careless of whose feelings I hurt and how savagely I hurt them." London's decision to involve himself and his reputation in the Marxist-Socialist labor movement was, in many respects, both brave and foolhardy. In doing so he endangered both his life and his income: there was the possibility of assassination, and also the possibility that certain magazines and certain publishers could blacklist him. But his very vocal membership in the Socialist Party also contributed greatly to his international popularity, and his willingness to talk revolution gave him the kind of heroic stature that his writing alone could not have achieved.

London had been involved in party activities for years, but the sudden success of *The Call of the Wild* in 1903, the rise of *The Sea-Wolf* to the top of the best-seller list in 1904, and the publication of his essay collection, *War of the Classes*, in 1905 made him extremely valuable as a spokesman for leftist causes. In the fall of 1905 the Slayton Lecture Bureau in Chicago arranged a lecture tour for him under the sponsorship of the Intercollegiate Socialist Society. Upton Sinclair, society founder and soon to be a controversial figure in his own right for his 1908 exposé of the Chicago meat-packing industry in *The Jungle*, was quick to realize that London, with his reputation as an adventurer, could attract audiences in places where other socialists could not get past the door.

London captivated listeners from Kansas City to New York with accounts of his experiences, sometimes read from his stories. But he always got around to his main point: his hatred for capitalism and his belief in the inevitability of the coming socialist revolution. The lecture tour did not run entirely smoothly, however. Several organizations canceled appearances after London married Charmian on November 19, only one day after his divorce was final and in apparent disregard of an Illinois law that required a one-year interval before remarriage. London answered that he would get married in every state in the Union, if necessary, and Illinois authorities decided to let the matter drop. But when he spoke at New York's Central Palace on January 19, 1906, and at Yale University on January 26, he received enormous acclaim, fueled in part by the headlines and editorials that appeared across the country proclaiming London a bigamist.

At the New York performance, hawkers sold red flags and red candy. Women made up two-thirds of the audience, many of them wearing red dresses or red ribbons in their hair, and several fainting when London arrived. The audience got what it came to hear: a celebrated author, fully as handsome as the newspaper pictures showed him to be, preaching fierce socialism in steady tones, vilifying capitalism, and claiming brotherhood with the Russian revolutionists. The lecture at Yale was made all the more dramatic by the uproar that followed the New York speech. Students awoke on January 26 to find posters showing London in a red sweater affixed to trees and notice boards all over the campus. London spoke to an audience of nearly three-thousand (probably including Yale student Sinclair Lewis) in Woolsey Hall. After the lecture, students carried him off to a dormitory, where he answered questions for hours.

Although London was not a dramatic speaker and did not pretend to be an entertainer, his lecture series was an enormous hit. One of the newspapers covering the Yale lecture preserved an impression of London's speaking style, reporting that "he walked to the edge of the stage and began to speak in a clear voice, which reached easily to the fartherest [sic] corner of the hall. He used scarcely any gestures, and rarely used his voice even to emphasize a point. His emphasis he got by reiteration."[40] London was at the top of his public acclaim as a controversial figure, so much so that libraries began passing resolutions to withdraw his books from circulation.

London had, of course, contributed greatly to his appeal as an authority on social problems by earlier establishing a reputation that he was a writer who would go anywhere, at any risk, to get his materials. His Klondike experiences were of course the most famous, but two times in the years from 1900–1905 he went off on adventures that took him first into the most notorious slum area in England and then to the rugged countryside of Korea.

Partly to escape from his marriage, but more practically because he was three thousand dollars in debt, he accepted an offer from the American Press Association in July 1902 to go to South Africa to cover the aftermath of the Boer War. His assignment was changed sometime along the way, however, and he made arrangements, with the approval of Macmillan, to go to England and do a sociological study of living conditions in the slums of the East End of London. His proposal was to put on old clothes, disguise himself as a down-and-out American sailor, and disappear into the world of the muggers, the tramps, and the hopeless inhabitants of the casual wards of the workhouses. His six-week descent was not that of a mere participant; he went as a writer intent on producing a shockingly accurate report, rented a clean room where he could go to organize his notes, and even took a camera with him (two-thirds of the photos in the resulting book are his). Although he avoids mentioning it in *The People of the Abyss*, which Macmillan published in 1903, he was assisted in his introduction to the East End by British Marxists (members of the Social Democratic Federation), who apparently found lodgings for him in the Flower and Dean Street area made infamous by Jack the Ripper. The federation also provided the official reports that London later cited in documenting the conditions he had observed.

The personal dangers London faced while work-

ing on *The People of the Abyss* and the genuine sympathy
he showed for the slum dwellers with whom he lived
and suffered did as much as anything to earn him his
reputation as a proletarian writer. The book, which
sold over twenty thousand copies, gained him international attention within the socialist movement and
earned him a place in the history of the "muckraking
era" alongside Ida Tarbell, Lincoln Steffens, and Jacob
A. Riis (whose *The Battle with the Slum* had been
published a year earlier, also by Macmillan).

London's Korean adventure did not lead to the
same kind of success, but again he demonstrated
the courage and determination that made him a good
journalist. In late 1903, just before the outbreak of
war between Japan and Russia, London had rushed
The Sea-Wolf to completion and had separated from his
wife. He was living by himself in a six-room flat on
Telegraph Avenue and was hard-pressed for cash (a
week before Christmas he had only twenty dollars in
the bank). When four separate news agencies put in
bids for his services during the coming war, he grabbed
the one that paid the most. That London would accept
an offer from William Randolph Hearst, whose magazines and newspapers made a fetish out of the idea that
Japan was planning to seize the American Far West
and "orientalize" it, might have seemed reprehensible:
London's objectivity as a reporter would be suspect.
But London himself dismissed such criticism with
scorn, saying that he had signed on with Hearst simply
because his was the best offer. Some of the pieces he
sent back, such as "The Sufferings of the Japanese," are
fine documentary journalism, and the doggedness with
which he pursued his stories soon became legendary
among the other correspondents who were covering the
war with him.

He sailed from San Francisco on January 7, 1904,
aboard the S.S. *Siberia*, reaching Tokyo on January 24.
Unwilling to wait for clearance with the other corre-

spondents loafing around the Imperial Bar, London took a train to Kobe on January 27, went to Nagasaki and then Moji, where he bought a ticket for Inchon, Korea. But before he could use the ticket, the Moji Water Police arrested him for snapping pictures in a forbidden military area. London was fined five yen and had his camera confiscated (it took the skillful intervention of Lloyd Griscom, the United States minister to Japan, to get it back). His next ploy was to go to Shimonoseki, where he got a third-class ticket, and in a few days he found himself stranded in Korea.

Undaunted, London "chartered" a sampan manned by three Koreans and made his way up Korea's west coast in freezing weather. With two other correspondents, he recruited thirteen men, rented eighteen ponies, and set off for the front through districts where most of the natives had never seen a foreigner. London did push far enough north to get a scoop: the only account of the first battle between the advancing Japanese and the Cossack scouts. But the correspondents who had been forced to remain in Tokyo promptly filed protests, and Japanese authorities returned London and his partners to Seoul, classifying them as security risks. London was prohibited from moving very far beyond the city walls, and for a time resigned himself to telling stories and drinking at Martin's Bar. On April 16 he was allowed to move out with the First Column of the Japanese Army, but his nearest approach to the fighting was when he was allowed to watch the easy Japanese victory at the Battle of the Yalu from long distance. (His dispatch of April 30 was, appropriately enough, entitled "Fighting at Long Range Described.")

While at the front, however, London got into trouble for striking a Japanese servant he caught stealing the fodder rations from the horses. London's action was a serious matter, given the racial tensions between the Japanese and the American correspondents, and he was hauled before General Fuji, the chief of staff, where there was talk of a firing squad. It took Richard Harding Davis, one of the most celebrated war reporters and author of the adventure novel *Soldiers of Fortune*, to save him. Davis cabled President Roosevelt from Japan and arranged a protest from the White House through the United States ministry to Tokyo. London was given an expulsion order, and he returned to San Francisco in July, his dangerous experiences contributing directly to the sensational reception of *The Sea-Wolf*, which had an advance sale of twenty thousand copies.

But Korea was not enough for London. He always was on edge for adventure, and he returned from the Orient with new plans. First would be the acquisition of some land where he could build a dream house for Charmian and himself. But before settling down, there would be the fulfillment of another dream: a seven-year voyage around the world in a ship he would design and have built to his specifications.

For several years, London had been vacationing at Wake Robin Lodge near the little town of Glen Ellen, fifty miles north of San Francisco. London liked to ride through the woods around Sonoma Mountain and the Valley of the Moon. When he learned that a small ranch of 129 acres, the old "Greenlaw Place," was for sale, he decided to buy it, paying seven thousand dollars for the land and another six hundred for the cows, horses, and machinery that went with it. On June 7, 1905, he wrote to George Brett at Macmillan and asked for ten thousand dollars against *The Sea-Wolf* and the story collection *The Faith of Men*, admitting that he had pinched his ready cash pretty much down and that he would be "flat-broke" until he got his remittance.[41] Brett was appalled. He was certain that it would be the ruin of London's career to take on such a long-term obligation, but the money was advanced, however reluctantly. London had protested that he had no intention of becoming a farmer, that he only wanted to make his home on the ranch, but soon he was reading books on scientific farming and beginning a series of costly experiments that included an advanced "piggery," the planting of eucalyptus trees to take advantage of a predicted boom in the use of the timber as dock-pilings, the acquisition of additional land (the ranch eventually encompassed 1,439 acres), and the building of Wolf House.

If Brett were not disturbed enough by London's June 7 letter, consider what he must have thought when he read the postscript to a letter dated August 1, in which London intimated that he had another big project in mind — a cruise around the world.[42] Brett by now had learned to take him at his word. Less than a year later, the keel of the *Snark* was laid (the name of the ship is a portmanteau word combining "snake" and "shark" in Lewis Carroll's mock-heroic poem "The Hunting of the Snark"), and London himself was launched on a mad push to meet expenses.

His sudden decisions were not always as impulsive as they might at first have seemed. He had been thinking of the *Snark* at least as early as 1903, or perhaps earlier when he read a book called *Sailing Alone Around the World* (1900) by a shipmaster named Joshua Slocum. There was to be one big difference between Slocum's adventure and London's, however. Slocum built his boat *The Spray* for $553.62; London would spend over $30,000 on the *Snark*, and it would be remembered around San Francisco Bay as "London's folly." But such an epithet is unfair. Despite all of the delays, all of the problems, and the ship's ignominious end in the Solomon Islands two years into the seven-year voyage as a "blackbirder" or slave ship, the *Snark* represented a new life for London, provided him with fresh material for some surprisingly good fiction, and gave him, when running before a good wind, some of the happiest moments of his life.

Once he made his decision concerning the *Snark*,

he began in typical London style — by reading the most advanced books on shipbuilding and engines. He would construct the strongest boat of its type, a forty-five-foot ketch, with a garboard strake three inches thick and two-inch planking, with a storm-punching strengthened bow, watertight bulkheads, and a seventy-horsepower Century engine for auxiliary power. The boat would have three staterooms, an engine room, head, and galley, and would be capable of ten knots under sail. No ballast would be necessary; the iron keel would weigh five tons. The design itself was not necessarily bad, but getting the ship built was a problem compounded by the great San Francisco earthquake of April 18, 1906, which not only toppled London's new barn at Glen Ellen, but sent the cost of labor and materials skyhigh. In order to finish the *Snark*, London had to deal with over forty unions and over a hundred firms. The result was to be expected: throughout the voyage London had to put up with a leaking hull, an unreliable and poorly mounted engine, bad handling characteristics, and dozens of other problems caused by shoddy workmanship.

But expense was the greatest problem of all. While he was designing and building the *Snark*, London was also putting thousands of dollars' worth of improvements into the ranch. He stepped up his daily thousand-word pace, and for a while he did some of his best writing. He completed *White Fang* (1906) in two months and sold the serial rights to *Outing* magazine for $7,500. He published two collections of stories, *Moon-Face and Other Stories* (1906) and *Love of Life and Other Stories* (1907); a play, *Scorn of Women* (1906); a children's book, *Tales of the Fish Patrol* (1905); a boxing novel, *The Game* (1905); a prehistoric fantasy, *Before Adam* (1907); and an account of his tramping experiences, *The Road* (1907). In addition to this truly fevered production, he began *The Iron Heel* in the summer of 1907, when the keel of the *Snark* was laid, and had the book finished by December. But even that was not enough. He planned to make the voyage pay for itself by offering magazines exclusive rights to his experiences. He signed a contract with *Cosmopolitan* for a travelogue, but later broke the contract. He offered to provide accounts of domestic life in the South Seas to *Woman's Home Companion*, and he presold a series of illustrated articles to *Collier's*. Despite all attempts at keeping up with his steadily inflating costs, London almost went bankrupt. He had to mortgage the house he had bought in Oakland for his mother, and sign away his future royalties. On the Saturday of his sailing, he was met at the wharf by a United States marshal serving a writ from an Oakland grocer attaching the ketch for an unpaid bill of $247.79. It was not until several days later (April 23, 1907) that the *Snark*, with London at the wheel, departed the Franklin Street wharf.

Even though he had repeated trouble with his crew (at almost every stop London had to fire somebody) and with the ship itself, London gloried in following in the wake of Herman Melville and Robert Louis Stevenson to the South Seas. The *Snark* stopped for refitting at Pearl Harbor, then set out for the Marquesas Islands with London charting a route that the *South Sea Directory* cautioned about even attempting—no sailing boat was known to have succeeded in making the crossing. London completed the challenge in sixty days. He stopped at Nuka Hiva, where Stevenson had lived, then rode out to the valley of Haapa, the setting for Melville's *Typee*.

But when the *Snark* reached Papeete in Tahiti and London could pick up the mail that had been forwarded to him, he learned that his checks had been bouncing and that he possessed only sixty-six dollars against gigantic liabilities. He had to book round-trip passage for himself and Charmian on the steamer *Mariposa* to return to California and get his accounts straightened out. He worked on completing the autobiographical *Martin Eden* (1909) on the way home, and managed to raise five thousand dollars from Macmillan on the strength of the novel. He also persuaded *Harper's* magazine to pay in advance for articles about the *Snark*. And on his return to Papeete, he learned that the serial rights to *Martin Eden* had been sold for seven thousand dollars. Once again, as he did so many times in his life, he had gone from near bankruptcy to shaky solvency in a matter of weeks.

The cruise of the *Snark* was resumed to the Fiji Islands and the Solomons, where London and his crew had their run-in with the bushmen when the *Snark* got caught on a reef and was attacked by cannibals. It was thus with some satisfaction that London went on a "blackbirding" expedition aboard another ship to see how the head-hunting cannibals were "recruited" as virtual slaves for plantation labor. It was also in the Solomons, however, that the *Snark* became a floating infirmary. First, it was malaria and blackwater fever. Then came "Solomon sores," or yaws, raspberry-like skin eruptions and destructive lesions caused by a tropical spirochete. London, who had up to eight of the lesions at a time, turned physician, treating himself and the crew with dangerous concoctions of blue vitriol and iodoform, lime juice and hydrogen peroxide, and boracic acid and lysol, all the while prescribing huge doses of quinine. He also came down with "sun sickness" caused by his sensitivity to ultraviolet light. His skin began flaking off, his hands puffed up, and he began to lose his coordination. He ordered the *Snark* to Guadalcanal, and he and Charmian took a steamer to Australia, where he was put into the Sidney Homeopathic Hospital. His skin slowly healed, but his doctors treated the yaws with an arsenic compound that may have damaged his kidneys and nerves. Continuing on the *Snark* was impossible for London, and he was forced to sell it at auction for three thousand dollars; it ended up in the New Hebrides as a transport ship for slave laborers.

London and Charmian nonetheless gamely tried to make their return voyage another adventure of sorts. They sailed to South America aboard the tramp collier *Tymeric* (getting a glimpse on the way of Pitcairn Island, made famous by the *Bounty* mutiny), stopped in Ecuador for a month, saw a bullfight, went alligator hunting, and continued to the Canal Zone, where they took passage on a United Fruit Company ship for New Orleans. They reached Oakland on July 24, 1909. The adventure that London had hoped would give him a new Yukon was over, and he was more in debt than ever.

But the South Seas did provide London with enough material for dozens of stories (collected in such volumes as the 1911 *South Seas Tales* and the posthumous *On the Makaloa Mat*, published in 1919), three novels, *Adventure* (1911), *Jerry of the Islands* (1917), and *Michael, Brother of Jerry* (1917), as well as the collection of articles that went into *The Cruise of the Snark* (1911). Even so, London was pressured into working more and liking it less, often losing his temper and proclaiming that he was writing only for money and always had been. When desperate, he even reverted to dog stories, which the regrettably bad *Jerry* and *Michael* are. But this last phase of his career has another side. With *Martin Eden* and *John Barleycorn* he turned to autobiography, the first book an intricate account of his development as a writer, the second a harrowing account of his life as an alcoholic. Together, the two—along with the earlier *The Road*—make up one of the best American contributions to a difficult genre. Although not always reliable as sources for biography (*good* autobiography perhaps never can be), they signal an introspective, foreboding tone in London's work and represent an attempt at summing things up before it was too late. *Martin Eden* ends with a suicide, *John Barleycorn* with an appeal for national prohibition; both offer sudden endings as solutions.

London himself saw his life as a landowner to be the best solution for the disappointments of the *Snark*. By the time he and Charmian returned to Glen Ellen, he was calling his property the "Beauty Ranch." What it meant to him is demonstrated in *Burning Daylight* (1910), a novel about a man who has made millions out of Alaska but whose personality had been nearly destroyed by the demands and corruptions of business. His secretary convinces him to settle on a little ranch in the Sonoma Hills, where he regains his health and ends his own "long sickness." Is there a difference between fact and fiction? In 1911 Western State Life Insurance Company turned London down as a bad health risk.

When Charmian told her husband during Christmas 1909 that she was pregnant, London renewed his hopes for a "London dynasty"—or at least one son—and decided that it was time to begin work on the dream house he and Charmian had talked about years before. The house was to be built, as much as possible, out of materials on the ranch. For earthquake protection, it would be put on a huge floating slab sufficient to support a forty-story building. Redwood trees, volcanic rocks, blue slate, and cement would be the building materials. The living room would be eighteen by fifty-eight feet and two stories high, London's study nineteen by forty, with a library of the same size under it. The cost would approach seventy thousand dollars. Before construction was actually under way, London learned that he had only five hundred dollars in the bank and was being pressed for immediate payment of a bill for eight hundred—and this at a time when he was earning well over fifty thousand a year. But he drove himself to work harder, even after the baby, a girl named Joy, born June 19, 1910, did not live two days. There was still hope for another child, a son, and London was determined that Wolf House would be built.

Big ideas were behind all of London's ambitions, and Beauty Ranch was no exception. He had once been an active socialist; now he saw himself as an agricultural radical. He stopped wearing the pressed flannels that had been part of his socialist image and took to wearing Baden-Powell wide-brimmed hats and riding boots — even when he went East. He sought rejuvenation through reclamation of the overworked and mismanaged acreage he had bought. He began building silos, terraces, and a brood barn, installed a liquid-manure tank, dammed a stream on the property, and experimented with new crops. He dreamed of ultimately expanding his ranch so that it would support thirty families and become an agricultural colony which in itself would provide a vision for the future of the American West and a means of redeeming modern California. To make all this possible, London turned again to books, magazines, pamphlets, and anything he could find that would provide him with new ideas that could be put to immediate use. He invited professors of agriculture from California-Davis out to the ranch to give him advice. But many of the theories for improvement, as promising as they seemed, simply did not work. He bought a champion shorthorn bull that soon suffered a broken neck. He designed a stone-floored piggery, but his pigs died of pneumonia. He tried to introduce the Shire mare into Sonoma, but the horse's hairy forelegs were no good in the wet clay of winter. And there was the unfortunate planting of the 250,000 eucalyptus trees, for which, as it turned out, no market existed.

London wrote two novels that deal directly with his ranching experience, and the difference between the two reflects a gradual disillusionment with his agricultural radicalism. In the first, *The Valley of the Moon* (1913), a laundress and a teamster, disgusted with urban working-class life, manage to buy a small ranch in the Valley of the Moon, where they become scientific farmers and achieve the "California dream" that had escaped their pioneer ancestors. But in the second novel, *The Little Lady of the Big House* (1916), Dick Forrest and his wife, Paula, who own and scientifically manage 250,000 acres, lead a strangely sterile life despite their personal physical beauty and Dick's reputation as the farm expert who wrote *Corn in California, Farm Bookkeeping,* and *Cover Crops for California*. As Kevin Starr writes in *Americans and the California Dream*, "for all their trumpeting of heroic possibilities, for all their consumption of food, sun, fun, and culture, the characters of London's last novel are dead in spirits and appetites."[43] The novel ends with Paula committing suicide, clad in her riding outfit.

The Little Lady of the Big House was begun, significantly enough, in 1913, a year of disasters for London. A drought followed by a grasshopper plague ruined his crops. In July he had an appendectomy and was told by the surgeon that his kidneys were deteriorating so fast that it was imperative to stop drinking and to abandon the habit of eating raw fish and meat. And in August, Wolf House, supposedly fireproof and built to last a thousand years, burned down before he and Charmian could move in. Although arson was suspected, the cause of the fire was never determined. Only the mortgage was insured, and London was over a hundred thousand dollars in debt. In the previous year, Charmian had suffered a miscarriage, and by the end of 1913 there was no longer any serious talk of rebuilding Wolf House. For the rest of his life, a plain farmhouse combined with an adjoining stone winery that was remodeled to include a living room, dining room, and kitchen would be London's home.

Like Mark Twain before him, London was tempted by get-rich-quick schemes. He lost ten thousand dollars on a pair of deals in 1913 involving Mexican land development and a fidelity loan company. A year

earlier he had invested in the "Millergraph," a new lith-
ographic process that proved impossible to promote.
He allowed the incorporation of a company to sell "Jack
London Grape Juice" so that he could get a high price
for his own grapes. The company went under and he
was sued for over forty thousand dollars by stockhold-
ers (the case never reached court). And he entered into
an arrangement with Hollywood director and producer
Hobart Bosworth to make a series of films, the first to
be *The Sea-Wolf*, with Bosworth as Wolf Larsen. Although the seven-reel production made film history in
that it was one of the first successful feature films to
come out of Hollywood, it was forced to compete
against two other versions, and London had to file a
lawsuit to establish that he owned the film rights to his
own work. In the process, he was instrumental, along
with Rex Beach, Booth Tarkington, Ellen Glasgow, and
other writers, in founding the Authors' League of
America to protect copyrights. Although many of London's books were eventually made into films, he was to
realize little of the "pot of money" he thought moving
pictures would provide. He was being pursued by cred-
itors on all sides, and even allowed his name and "before and after" pictures of himself to be used in an
advertisement for the Royal Tailors of New York that
appeared in *Cosmopolitan* for November 1913. "It's funny
what a difference a few clothes make!" reads the copy.

London's money problems have usually been attributed to his spending on the *Snark*, the Beauty
Ranch, and Wolf House, but he had other heavy expenses as well in that he was supporting three additional households — those of his mother, Bess and his
daughters, and his stepsister Eliza — besides his own.
London was also exceptionally generous when it came
to giving loans to old friends, outright handouts to men
he had met during his adventures (many of the bums
from his hobo days arranged their travels to include

Glen Ellen), and aid of various sorts to young writers (such as buying plots he did not need from Sinclair Lewis, who never understood that situations, not plot lines, were what generated London's fiction). He was so open in welcoming visitors to the ranch that he had to have a circular printed to warn people that he worked mornings and could not see guests until the afternoon. When he did see them — and as often as not he had a dozen people at the dinner table — he talked openly and good-naturedly, and the dark moods that show up in his writing seldom appear in the memoirs others have written of him during his years of heaviest debt and hardest work.

His generosity also extended to the employees on his ranch, something for which he is still remembered around Glen Ellen. He often made a policy of hiring men just released from jail, and he tried never to turn down hungry men who showed up looking for work. His generosity was not always repaid, and many times he was charged for hours not worked and materials not bought. It is said that, in the three years Wolf House was under construction, London never lost his temper at the slow pace of the work. The Italian stonemason who was in charge of working the volcanic rock said that London was the best man he had ever met.[44]

As pressured as he was in his last years, London never lost his love of excitement, his craving for adventure. He had bought the *Roamer*, a thirty-foot yawl, in 1910, and he and Charmian and friends would go for long cruises up Bay or down. In 1911, he and Charmian hitched four horses to their Studebaker wagon and took a three-month, fifteen-hundred-mile trip from Glen Ellen through the mountains of northern California to Oregon and back. In 1912, with the idea of experiencing what the old Californians had gone through, he and Charmian sailed from Baltimore around the horn on the clipper *Dirigo*. And he continued to make big plans for new books (*My Great Labor Novel* was one projected title), more acreage, and another boat — a three-topmast schooner with space aboard for a grand piano, a launch, and a touring car. With a doctor, servants, and crew, London and Charmian would wander the seas for years. "I never saw a man in all my life with more magnetism, beautiful magnetism," London's friend, the sculptor Finn Froleich, asserted. "If a preacher could have the love in his make-up, and the life, God, this whole world would go religious."[45]

But mere plans were never enough for London. He remained ready to take on an exciting assignment, and when President Wilson sent a military force to Veracruz in the spring of 1914 to protect American citizens and interests during the long-running Mexican Revolution, London was again eager to turn war correspondent. He first tried to get an assignment from Hearst, but when *Collier's* offered him eleven hundred dollars a week and expenses, he accepted at once.

The battle of Veracruz took place on April 21, before London could reach the city. American marines, supported by the guns of the U.S.S. *Prairie*, took the city at a cost of 19 American and 126 Mexican lives, and some American newspapers began raising the cry "On to Mexico City!" When London, accompanied by Charmian and his valet, reached Galveston, Texas, where he was to receive his credentials, he learned that his papers were being withheld on the commanding general's orders. The general was angry at London because of an antimilitary diatribe, "The Good Soldier," that London supposedly had written for the *International Socialist Review*. London claimed that the essay was a forgery, but the general refused to believe him until Richard Harding Davis and other correspondents intervened. The Army and the Navy cleared London of authorship of the notorious article in 1916. After London's death, Theodore Roosevelt wrote to Charmian saying that he was convinced of London's innocence in the matter.

Whether or not London had actually written "The Good Soldier," the general had nothing to worry about. The dispatches London sent back strongly supported American intervention. London wrote that Veracruz under American military occupation was a cleaner, more decent city than it had ever been, and that the American oil men at the nearby Tampico oil fields were to be praised for developing resources of enormous potential benefit to both the United States and Mexico. He went so far as to point out that the enterprising business atmosphere at Tampico reminded him of the Klondike.

All of this was shocking to the Socialist Party, which had denounced the intervention and the American exploitation of the oil fields. It was doubly shocking because London had written an open letter in February 1911 attacking the grafters and large landowners and indicating his general support of the Mexican revolutionaries. He had also written a short story, "The Mexican," in 1911 in which a boxer beats a cheating gringo opponent and uses the prize money to buy guns for the revolution. Even before London's first articles appeared in *Collier's*, it was rumored that he had gone to join the rebels (a newspaper actually published a headline, "Jack London Leads Army of Mexican Rebels," and it was reported that he had been wounded in action). London's dispatches thus seemed like a tragic sellout to his radical followers and damaged his reputation for years after his death. "My boyhood's Socialist hero, Jack London, had died in 1916, no hero any longer in my eyes," Floyd Dell, American leftist and novelist, wrote in 1933. "A few years earlier, sent to Mexico as a correspondent, he came back singing the tunes that had been taught him by the oil men who were engaged in looting Mexico; he preached Nordic supremacy, and the manifest destiny of the American exploiters. He had apparently lost faith in the revolution in which he had once believed."[40]

But London's time in Mexico needs to be put into perspective. When the Mexican Revolution broke out in late 1910 and early 1911, it was hailed by socialists and anarchists as an opening episode in the coming world revolution. But by 1914 it had gotten so confused that it was impossible to tell what was going on among the competing factions: the Federal troops under Huerta, the Constitutionalists under Carranza and Obregón in the east, the hard-riding *guerrilleros* of the north, and Zapata's rebel peons in the south. American investment in Mexico had been heavy (London himself was involved in a land company) and Americans were being attacked on the streets. Even more troublesome was the involvement of Japan and Germany. At a time when it was apparent to many that world war was inevitable, Japan openly challenged American policy by supplying Huerta with guns and munitions. The Germans were also supporting Huerta and had dispatched a freighter loaded with weapons to Veracruz. The occupation of the city took place the day before the freighter was due to arrive, and although the ship was prevented from unloading, it and another German supply ship were able to steam down the coast and unload at Puerta Mexico. London understood that what was happening was anything but a genuine revolution of the working class and that the real issue involving Mexico and the United States had worldwide implications going beyond socialist objections to "naked imperialism." Subsequent events proved him right. By 1916 the Union of German Citizens had twenty-two branches in Mexico, in addition to the seventy-five chapters of the Iron Cross Society, and there were reports that the German and Austrian consuls were providing support for an army that was preparing to attack Texas. And on January 16, 1917, British intelligence intercepted a German cable proposing an alliance with Mexico that would throw German support behind the reconquest of lost territory in Texas, New Mexico, and Arizona.

Despite the controversy resulting from his Mexican articles, London's stay in Mexico was brief. He caught amoebic dysentery, complicated by pleurisy, and almost died in the hospital at Veracruz. He and Charmian returned to Galveston on a cattle boat and got back to Glen Ellen in mid-June. A few days later, he wrote a letter to Ralph Kasper, a close socialist friend, confessing a belief in hopeless materialism and despairing of any hope for the immortality of the human soul. At the time of his death, London would be as much obliterated as the last insect he had squashed.[47] This had always been his belief, London explained, and the nearly fatal conclusion to his Mexican adventure had reinforced it.

He began speaking of himself as "the ancient," and he astonished his friends, most of them also still in their thirties, by referring to all present as "We oldsters." And almost as if he were taking premature retirement, he and Charmian spent twelve of his last eighteen months on Hawaii. There was no pretense of adventure this time, simply a leisured life (once the daily thousand words were written) and escape from his difficulties. He worked more steadily than he ever had at slowly relieving his load of debts by keeping expenses at the ranch to a minimum and allowing Wolf House to lie in ruins.

His retreat to Hawaii was accompanied by his withdrawal from the socialist movement. When he made formal his resignation from the Socialist Party in a letter written March 27, 1916, his socialist critics simply assumed the worst: that his obsession with money and property had finally gotten the best of him. But London's resignation was not unexpected, and the fact was that by 1916 the Great War had pretty much splintered international socialism.

At the outset of the war, London was appalled that the German socialists, who made up the most powerful socialist party in the world, had thrown their support behind the Kaiser in a conflict London clearly saw as one between barbarism and civilization, not between labor and capital. He had long argued that socialism would make war impossible, and in *The Iron Heel* he had a general strike of the workers stop a war between Germany and America. But in real life, German socialists and American socialists had shown they could no longer cooperate, and even within the Socialist Party in the United States there were disagreements concerning proper response to the war. Some members, such as Eugene Debs, advocated pacifism in favor of the future revolution, while others supported the allied cause with the same intensity that their German comrades were backing the Kaiser.

Given the way the German socialists had betrayed the international cause, London did not see how American socialists could oppose American involvement in the war. To London, the leaders of the party were to be pitied for their lack of courage and their inability to see the betrayal of their own idealism. He felt he had given a quarter of a century of his life to the revolutionary movement only to see much of what he fought for simply disregarded. But it is a mistake to believe that in writing his letter of resignation he gave up his belief in socialist principles; it was simply that he could no longer find a place for himself in the movement. "Instead of resigning," writes Philip S. Foner in *Jack London: American Rebel*,

London could have thrown in his lot with the left wing forces who shared his conviction that the Party had lost its militancy and joined them in seeking to check compromise tendencies and build a truly revolutionary movement. Yet the tragedy of

London's position was that he no longer fitted anywhere in the movement. If his beliefs in revolutionary socialism made it impossible for him to work with the conservative socialists, his attitude towards the World War which had broken out in the summer of 1914 made it equally impossible for him, had he wished to do so, to cooperate with the left-wing socialists.[48]

After his death, socialist journals attributed his resignation to his state of health and most of them simply went on referring to him as "Comrade Jack London."

By 1916, London's various ailments, all complicated by his failing kidneys, had prematurely aged him. His gums were swollen with pyorrhea, his feet and ankles were puffed up with edema, and his "cast-iron" stomach began rejecting his meals of raw fish and meat. In September he decided to ignore the advice of his doctors and try to subsist on two undercooked wild ducks a day. By early November he was passing matter in his urine. On November 10, food poisoning led to dysentery. On Tuesday, November 21, he was forced to stay in bed until late afternoon. After dinner, he rested with Charmian for an hour, and then went to his room, carrying the two wooden box-trays of books and magazines that he took to bed with him most nights. He stretched out and made some notes about a "socialist autobiography" and a novel about the Vikings in North America, then wrote a letter to his daughter Joan about an outing he had planned for her and her sister the next Sunday. He opened a book, *Around Cape Horn, Maine to California in 1852*, read a few pages and then marked his place with a dead match. Sometime during the night he injected himself with at least twelve and a half grains of morphine sulfate mixed with atropine sulfate to relieve the pain his kidneys were causing him. When his Japanese houseboy brought coffee at seven o'clock the next morning, London was lying doubled-up, breathing heavily, his face purple.

A doctor from Sonoma was the first to arrive, and

he later claimed that London had left some calculations on his night table. The doctor assumed the figure represented an attempt at working out a lethal dose of morphine, but most likely they were merely numbers relating to royalty percentages; no one else but the Sonoma doctor recalled seeing the pad of paper on which the figures were written. He also said he found two empty drug phials on the floor, and that is why he began immediate treatment for an overdose of morphine accompanied by renal colic. Two specialists from Oakland and San Francisco were called in, but London did not come out of his coma. At 7:45 P.M. he died. The cause of death announced to the public was "uremia following renal colic."

Rumors of suicide were inevitable, and Irving Stone tried to confirm them in *Sailor on Horseback*, writing that London deliberately murdered himself with a drug overdose. But most of the evidence now points the other way: that London died essentially of natural causes.[49] Drugs certainly were an increasing part of London's life as his pathological disease worsened. He had been taking opiate medicines liberally for a year or more prior to his death, and he had built up a tolerance to the drugs — which is understandable enough, given the excruciating pain caused by renal colic. Extreme suffering often does lead to excessive, sometimes inadvertent measures in self-medication. London's case was a complicated one, and alcohol (he probably had had a cocktail or two before dinner) could have reinforced the depressant effects of morphine so that an otherwise safe dosage could prove fatally dangerous to an already weakened system.

But the biggest problem with the suicide-by-morphine theory is that morphine is simply not a very good agent for self-destruction. It is slow, and not at all what someone like London, who had thirty-six heavily annotated medical books in his library, would choose. Besides, he had a faster, surer way close at hand: the loaded forty-four caliber Colt revolver he always kept within easy reach of his bed. At any rate, suicide by whatever means seems an unlikely choice for London to have made. The day before his death, he was full of plans: the outing with his daughters, a trip to New York and then to Scandinavia, more stories, essays, and books. And despite the terrors that were the consequence of his bad health, several friends reported that he was still capable of exuding his well-known vitality and essential cheerfulness right down to his final days. Jack London may have lived recklessly, pushing self-destructive habits to the maximum, but most likely he was not a suicide.

His body, in a small gray coffin, lay in state in his study until Friday, when it was taken to Oakland for a simple funeral service that included a reading of William Cullen Bryant's "Thanatopsis" and a short memorial poem by George Sterling, which ended with the line ". . . and a soul like thine — how shall it die?" On Sunday, Sterling brought the urn containing London's ashes to the ranch, where they were buried on a little knoll. A huge red boulder that the builders of Wolf House had had to reject because of its size was levered into place over the grave.

The demand for London's books did not stop with his death, and at least twelve volumes (one as late as 1972) were published posthumously in English. His popularity, particularly abroad, has diminished little, and London remains the best-selling American writer worldwide. Nearly eight million copies of *The Call of the Wild* have been sold since 1903, his work has been translated into over sixty languages, and in the Soviet Union there are nine separate editions of his collected work. For years, however, London received uncertain critical praise in his own country, partly because he proclaimed too openly that he was writing for money — that he was

strictly a "commercial" writer — and partly because he
was classified, at best, as an author of books for boys,
about dogs. Perhaps most damaging, however, was the
tendency to think of London as some sort of "natural
genius." Although very sympathetic to London's work,
even H.L. Mencken took this tack in his 1919 eulogy of
him. "Where did he get his hot artistic passion, his
delicate feeling for form and color, his extraordinary
skill with words?" Mencken asked. "The man in truth
was an instinctive artist of a high order, and if igno-
rance often corrupted his art, it only made the fact of
his inborn mastery more remarkable."[50] Mencken was
right on one point: London did have extraordinary skill
as a writer. But Mencken was utterly wrong on another
point: London was one of the least ignorant of writers,
and his best stuff is always as much dependent on his
extensive reading and his powerful scholar's curiosity as
it is on his instinctive artistry and his action-packed
life.

London was constantly on the lookout for new
ideas, and in the last phase of his intellectual life he
began a study of Sigmund Freud and Carl Jung with
the thought that they might give his fiction a new direction. After reading Jung's *Psychology of the Unconscious*,
London said to Charmian, "Mate Woman, I tell you I
am standing on the edge of a world so new, so terrible,
so wonderful, that I am almost afraid to look over into
it."[51] London did not live long enough to make much
use of these new concepts, but, if he had, it is probable — given his eagerness to incorporate new ideas into
his fiction — that he would have become that rarest of
writers, one who could transcend his own literary era
and move confidently into the alien world of modern-
ism.

This did not quite happen, but London's remarkable variety of work has survived intact through several
changes in literary fashion that are now themselves

dead and gone, while much of his writing remains full of life. Jack London's voice is a strong one, a sure one, hauntingly contemporary to successive generations of readers, who have realized that the letter of inquiry he sent to the editor of the San Francisco *Bulletin* upon returning from the Klondike in 1898 is ultimately addressed to them. "I have sailed and traveled quite extensively in other parts of the world and have learned to seize upon that which is interesting," London wrote, "to grasp the true romance of things, and to understand the people I may be thrown against."[32]

2

Meditations on Man
and Beast

"As for the hardship," Jack London wrote concerning
his experiences in the Klondike and Alaska,

it cannot be conveyed by printed page or word of mouth. No
man may know who has not undergone. And those who have
undergone, out of their knowledge, claim that in the making
of the world God grew tired, and when He came to the last
barrowload, "just dumped in anyhow," and that was how
Alaska happened to be.[1]

This is a strange statement, given the source: a writer
who profited enormously from the stories he wrote
about the White Silence of the Northland, and who
confessed, concerning his greatest and most famous
adventure, "I never realized a cent from any properties
I had an interest in up there. Still I have been manag-
ing to pan out a living ever since on the strength of the
trip."[2]

London devoted so many pages to the great gold
rush of 1897 and talked about it so much in his lectures
that accounts of his supposed exploits — such as shooting the Mane of the White Horse Rapids — are still
being told in the saloons of Dawson, and more than
one old-timer over the years has claimed to be his long-
lost son. But as willing as London always was to profit
from the romantic lore that made him out to be so

much more than he actually was—for the most part, just another sourdough who spent a miserable winter on Split-Up Island—he had no illusions about his Klondike stories. He did not write them as documentary narratives; he wrote them as meditations on what happens to men and beasts when they are thrust into "the Wild, the savage, frozen-hearted Northland Wild," as he terms it in *White Fang*.

The Northland, as London experienced it from the moment he set foot on Dyea beach, was a Darwinian nightmare. The screaming horses, the arguments over tangled gear, the fistfights, and the distant sound of scores being settled with drawn revolvers could only have confirmed the evolutionary survival-of-the-fittest theories that were already embedded in his deepest consciousness. Within a few days he and his partners were reduced to pack animals as they lugged and sweated their outfits up and over Chilkoot Pass. Their journey through the lakes and rivers to Dawson seemed to be taking them to the "unprotected tip of the planet," and that winter London would lie on his bunk in a tiny cabin at the confluence of two frozen rivers and think about the sudden death that waited for him at seventy-five degrees below zero just outside the door. His respect for the men who could actually thrive in such an environment gradually overwhelmed his imagination. He began to see them as emblematic figures who had somehow developed a code of behavior that would enable them to endure life at the very limits of existence. Some of these men he had met at the Moosehorn Bar and the Elkhorn Saloon in Dawson the previous fall, men with nicknames like "Slackwater," "Siwash," and "Axe-handle." Others had stopped for a rest at Split-Up Island, where they accepted steaming mugs of tea and told stories about running the "Saltwater Mail" to Skagway with wolves howling around them all the way. The wolves themselves were topics of conversation, as were the sled dogs the mushers talked about as if each dog possessed a human personality. London may even have heard a tale about a giant husky that had gone wild and turned into a "Ghost Dog."

London did not spend much time — if any — working his claim on Henderson Creek. And as far as is known, he did not do any writing until he began the diary he kept of his float down the Yukon on his way out. But when he returned to Oakland and began to compose the cycle of Northland stories that begins with "To the Man on Trail" and culminates in *The Call of the Wild*, he had developed a vision of the Klondike as an enormous laboratory of red-blooded adventure, where his characters could be reduced to "primordial simplicity" as they learn the frostbitten truth about the Law of Life. Survival for both man and beast in such an environment depended on the successful adoption of instinctive codes of behavior that often obscured the differences between men and animals.

man and beast

As London thought about what he had heard and seen in the Northland, the nicknamed men of the Dawson saloons worked their way through his imagination and emerged as the Malemute Kid and Sitka Charley. The Ghost Dog turned into Buck, and out of the wolf pack came White Fang. These characters exist to teach the essential lesson that runs through all of the Klondike stories: "When a man journeys into a far country, he must be prepared to forget many of the things he has learned, and to acquire such customs as are inherent with existence in the new land; he must abandon the old ideals and the old gods, and oftentimes he must reverse the very codes by which his conduct has hitherto been shaped."[3]

London claimed to have taken two books with him when he left Oakland in July 1897: Spencer's *Philosophy of Style* and Milton's *Paradise Lost*. For one who presumes to make pronouncements about effective writing, Spencer himself is anything but easy to read. But when reading matter is scarce — as it most certainly was on Split-Up Island — men will do strange things. Spencer's actual recommendations, however, are fairly simple, and it is easy enough to see how they had a lasting influence on London. Spencer's first concern was for the reader, a rather passive soul who had only so much mental energy at the writer's disposal. The trick was for the writer to conserve this pool of energy by using common words and simplified sentence structure to get the reader's energy flowing in the right direction: toward the comprehension of the idea or emotion the writer has in mind. Complexity, whether in plot, language, or character, is to be avoided. The last thing the writer wants to do is to waste the reader's energy. Simple language is the best tool for conveying each thought, step by step, into the reader's mind. What London liked most about Spencer's philosophy of style was that it seemed scientific. London, of course, did not always practice what Spencer rather dully preached, and London's style at any moment appears ready to explode — and often does — into Biblically allegorical rhetoric.

This perhaps explains the presence of the other book in London's pack. *Paradise Lost* has an impact on the entire Northland cycle of stories and novels. Most of London's characters are like Milton's fallen angels. They are either outcasts or egotists who have abandoned the golden climes of the Southland to seek their fortunes and their freedom in the Klondike or Alaska. Many of them, like Milton's Lucifer, are pledged to a lost cause, hurled into the hell of the White Silence, yet refuse to be beaten. The Malemute Kid, the central figure in *The Son of the Wolf*, is one of these fallen angels. London never has the Kid reveal how he got to the Northland or when he intends to leave; it is as if the Kid has been condemned to the frozen wasteland forever. Like Milton's Lucifer, the Kid is fully aware of what it means to be there, and resolves to make a heaven of hell. And it is precisely this that the Kid is doing as the first of the Klondike stories, "To the Man on Trail," opens.

London's Klondike stories are all meditations on the idea of adaptability and change, and "To the Man on Trail," the first of the Klondike stories to be published by the *Overland Monthly* (January 1899) is a good example. It also introduces ideas that show up repeatedly in the other stories.

On Christmas Eve, the Malemute Kid concocts a powerful punch of whiskey, brandy, grain alcohol, and pepper-sauce for his friends in his cabin on Split-Up Island. A "born raconteur," the Kid joins in the round of stories and songs inspired by his "frightful concoction." At midnight the crunch of a dogsled is heard as it draws up to the cabin, and a stranger enters. He stands six-foot-two or -three, wears two Colt revolvers and a hunting knife on a beaded belt, and carries a smokeless rifle of the largest bore. He is so covered with ice that he looks like the Frost King. The stranger's name is Westondale, and he says he has been on the trail twelve hours running, in pursuit of a gang of dog thieves. After giving him a quick meal of bacon and moose-meat, the Kid shows Westondale to a bunk, promising to wake him in four hours. While Westondale sleeps, the Kid loads his sled with a hundred pounds of salmon eggs for dog food, and has the team harnessed and ready for the start when he rouses his guest. Telling him, "Watch out for open water on the Thirty Mile River, and be sure to take the big cut-off above Le Barge," the Kid sends him off. Fifteen minutes later, a Mountie, followed by two half-breed dog drivers, stumbles into the cabin and begins asking questions about Westondale. A quick glance from the Kid is enough to make his friends hesitate in answering. The Mountie tells them that Westondale has robbed a Dawson casino of forty thousand dollars, but no one moves to offer information to the officer. He asks for fresh dogs, but the Kid simply shakes his head.

The men all know that the lawman, with his tired dog team, has no chance of catching his man, and after the officer leaves they turn on the Kid. Even though part of their code is that they had to respect the Kid's signal that they remain silent, they cannot understand why he would help a man who had lied to them about the dog thieves and had betrayed the "ethics of the Northland, where honesty, above all, was man's prime jewel." The Kid pours himself a final round of punch and tells them, "It's a cold night, boys — a bitter cold night. You've all traveled trail, and know what that stands for. Don't jump a dog when he's down." He explains that they know only one side of the story, not the side the Kid had earlier heard from the Indian musher Sitka Charley.

The previous fall, Westondale had given his entire "clean-up" of forty thousand dollars to his partner Joe Castrell to buy in on another claim that would have made them both millionaires. But while Westondale stayed behind at Circle city caring for another partner who had scurvy, Castrell went into McFarland's casino, jumped the limit, and lost the whole sack. Castrell was found dead in the snow the next day. Westondale had planned to leave the gold fields, as soon as his investment paid off, to return to his wife and a son he had never seen. "You'll notice he took exactly what his partner lost — forty thousand," the Kid says. "Well, he's gone out; and what are you going to do about it?" The men's faces soften in the realization that Westondale has shown them another dimension of the code of the Northland. The story ends with a toast "to the man on trail this night," followed by the clicking of empty cups as someone shouts, "Confusion to the Mounted Police!"

London was fond of nicknames, and it is apparent

enough that he saw himself in the Malemute Kid. The very name suggests London's basic conception of human nature: part wild wolf, part domesticated dog, part human. The Kid figures in seven of the nine tales collected in *The Son of the Wolf*. "I may learn to love him too well myself," London said of the Kid in a letter to a friend. "I am afraid I am rather stuck on him — not on the one in print, but the one in my brain."[4]

The Kid's origins are never given, and there are no references to his family, not even a mention of a hometown. What he has learned in the Northland constitutes his entire personality, and he has been transformed by the Law of Life as he has learned it on a thousand frozen trails. The Kid has lived on rabbit tracks and salmon-belly, he has often faced sudden danger and quick death, and he can fell an ox with a single blow. He is enormously resourceful. He knows how a heat reflector built out of canvas can save a life in a pinch. He has great respect for animals, and never beats his sled dogs the way other drivers do. He never forgets the essential indifference of nature to man, but he always acts as if human life means more than mere survival. His friends are all hard-bitten men who, like him, know the Wisdom of the Trail: the Indian, Sitka Charley; the Jesuit Father, Roubeau; and the big and silent French-Canadian, Louis Savoy. In "The Wife of a King," the Kid even takes on the status of secular priest of the wilderness when he hears Father Roubeau's confession. The Kid always teaches one lesson: good men know they will die. The only just response is honesty, self-sacrifice, and faithful friendship.

But the Malemute Kid is not a mere giver of lessons. In several of the stories he demonstrates how he has come to learn the truth about man's place in the Northland. The best of these stories is "The White Silence," in which the Kid is accompanying a prospector named Mason and his Indian wife, Ruth, on a winter

trek to an unnamed destination. They have two hundred miles of unbroken trail ahead, and their dogs are
in bad shape. As Mason, Ruth, and the Kid push on
through an afternoon of heartbreaking labor, we discover the central force in the shaping of the Kid's character. London writes:

Nature has many tricks wherewith she convinces man of his
finity — the ceaseless flow of the tides, the fury of the storm,
the shock of the earthquake, the long roll of heaven's artil-
lery — but the most tremendous, the most stupefying of all, is
the passive phase of the White Silence. All movement ceases,
the sky clears, the heavens are as brass; the slightest whisper
seems sacrilege, and man becomes timid, affrighted at the
sound of his own voice. Sole speck of life journeying across
the ghostly wastes of a dead world, he trembles at his audaci-
ty, realizes that his is a maggot's life, nothing more.

The White Silence, the confrontation with absolute
nothingness — this is what the Kid has faced. He has
learned to survive in it and with it, but it has changed
him permanently. It is in the presence of the White
Silence that "the fear of death, of God, of the universe,
comes over him — the hope of the Resurrection and the
Life, the yearning for immortality, the vain striving of
the imprisoned essence — it is then, if ever, man walks
alone with God." But the walk is never a comforting
one.
    As Mason toils at the head of the pitiful cavalcade,
a giant pine that had stood beside the trail for generations crashes down on him. "The sudden danger, the
quick death — how often had Malemute Kid faced it!"
London interjects. "The pine needles were still quiver-
ing as he gave his commands and sprang into action."
The Kid and Ruth manage to pry the tree off Mason,
but it is sixty-five below zero and he is terribly crushed.
They build a fire and spend the night beside him. In
the morning he asks that they push on without him, but

the Kid insists that they will wait at least one more day. When the Kid returns from a hopeless attempt at finding some game, he discovers Ruth holding off the snarling sled dogs with an ax. The Kid joins in with his rifle butt, and "the hoary game of natural selection was played out with all the ruthlessness of its primeval environment." But the whole stock of dried salmon has been eaten, and they have only five pounds of flour left for the remaining two hundred miles of wilderness.

The next morning, the Kid bends the tops of several pines to the ground, fastens them down with moosehide, and builds a cradle for Mason by lashing his fur robes to the trees. The Kid allows Ruth one last outburst of grief, and sends her off with the foremost sled. Mason falls into a coma, but by high noon he is still alive. The Kid walks over to him and then looks around. "The White Silence seemed to sneer, and a great fear came upon him," London writes. "There was a sharp report; Mason swung into his aerial sepulchre; and Malemute Kid lashed the dogs into a wild gallop as he fled across the snow."

When the Kid shoots Mason, it would seem that he is betraying his belief in the idea of self-sacrificing friendship. But an essential part of the Northland code is adaptability. The White Silence, in its absolute indifference, "sneers" at all human attempts to understand it. Why should the tree have fallen on Mason? The Kid has no answer to that question, but he knows he cannot wait any longer if he is to get Ruth out to have the baby she is expecting. "Take care of her, Kid," Mason had told him. The Kid has only one choice: to preserve life, he must end a life, although he does not know why he has been brought to such a choice. He simply does what he must do. In a statement that serves as an oblique commentary on the Kid's action, London once suggested that the human dilemma is compounded by a generalized failure to realize "the utter absurdity, logically, of the finite contemplating the infinite."[5] This absurdity is what the Kid understands when the "great fear came upon him." Realizing the futility of asking why he must do it, he pulls the trigger and flees in horror across the snow.

"Only in man is morality," London writes in *John Barley-corn*, "and man created it — a code of action that makes toward living." The code demanded by the Northland is an extreme one, a desperate one, and those who fail to adapt, the way the Kid has, are soon destroyed by the White Silence. This is the point of "In a Far Country," one of the stories in *The Son of the Wolf* in which the Kid plays no part.

Two men, Carter Weatherbee and Percy Cuthfert, are "Incapables." They have contracted with two guides to take them into "the Unknown Lands," but Weather-bee and Cuthfert are unable to adapt to the demands of the trail and decide to spend the winter by themselves in a remote cabin rather than push on to the end of the journey. Lacking any sense of the code, unwilling to exercise any discipline in their eating habits, and unable to develop the kind of comradeship that would enable them to talk about their mutual "Fear of the North," they end by killing one another. Without the kind of morality represented by the Kid, characters in the Klondike stories simply fall apart, as one of the later stories, "To Build a Fire," included in the 1910 volume, *Lost Face*, agonizingly reveals.

"To Build a Fire" is a meditation "upon man's frailty in general, able only to live within narrow limits of heat and cold." Even though he is told by an old-timer in Sulphur Creek that the absolute law of travel in the Klondike is that no man should go out on the trail alone when the temperature drops under fifty below zero, a newcomer, or *chechaquo*, disregards the advice. Accompanied only by a dog, the temperature standing at seventy-five below, the young man falls through a spring hole in the ice of a creek and soaks himself

halfway to his knees. He has no choice if he is to survive: he must build a fire and dry out his footgear.
London comments on his character's predicament in
one sure sentence: "The cold of space smote the unprotected tip of the planet, and he, being on that unprotected tip, received the full force of the blow."

He gets a fire going, but he makes the mistake of
building it under a snow-laden spruce tree. An avalanche of snow falls from the tree and blots out the fire.
He tries again, but his fingers are too numb to hold the
matches. He thinks of killing the dog to warm his hands
in the carcass, but the dog senses the strange urgency
in his master's voice and refuses to come to him. Even
when he manages to grab the dog, he realizes he has no
way of holding his sheath knife, and his hands are too
weak for a stranglehold. He gets to his feet and tries to
run the remaining distance to the cabin on the left fork
of Henderson Creek, where his partners are waiting for
him, but he lacks the endurance to run that far. After
he falls for the second time, he resolves to face death
decently. "Freezing was not so bad as people thought,"
he reflects in one of London's most famous lines.
"There were lots worse ways to die." The dog waits until
he catches the "scent of death," and then trots up the
trail to the camp. London again makes clear his lesson
on "the conjectural field of immortality and man's place
in the universe."

This is the London story that is most often anthol-
ogized, and in mood and atmosphere—achieved
through the repetition of imagery associated with the
cold and gloom of the White Silence that envelops the
lonely traveler—it is starkly elegant, a masterpiece of
quiet tone and subdued color that immediately convinces the reader of "the strangeness and weirdness of it
all." It is, however, oddly without suspense. The protagonist is doomed from the first clause—"Day had broken
cold and gray"—and he cannot possibly get back to his
cabin. London's grim, choruslike voice reminds us of

this in a series of deadpan pronouncements on the unnamed hero's personality. "The trouble with him was
that he was without imagination," London observes in
the most important of these pronouncements. "He was
quick and alert in the things of life, but only in the
things, and not in the significances." He is utterly unlike the Malemute Kid in this regard, and is one of a
number of London's heroes who crack under the pres-
sures of their own existence because they have failed to
develop the most essential philosophy of life, that which
makes possible cheerful survival in an indifferent cosmos.

The Malemute Kid is a major character only in
London's first collection of stories, but he was resur-
rected years later as Smoke Bellew when *Cosmopolitan*
wanted a set of stories that would center on one character in the way that *The Son of the Wolf* had centered on the
Kid. Smoke Bellew is a San Francisco journalist, and
the early episodes show him following London's trail
over the Chilkoot to Dawson, where he soon develops
attitudes that are essentially similar to those of the Kid.
London wrote many of the Smoke Bellew stories (collected in 1912) as fast as possible, to bring in money for
the *Snark*, and some of them, such as "Meat" in the way
it imitates "In a Far Country," come close to self-parody.
London squandered his creative energies on Smoke
Bellew, but many of the stories are often humorous and
full of spirit, and the last story in the collection, "Wonder of Women," although overwritten, is one of his best
code-of-the-Northland stories. Smoke Bellew travels into an unmapped territory where he encounters the Indian girl Labiskwee. The two nearly go mad when they
get lost in a type of storm known as the "white death."
Snow-blinded, Smoke discovers that Labiskwee has
saved scraps of food for him out of her own starvation
share of their rations so that he will survive, even if it
means her own death.

Women often play an important part in the Klondike stories, and the women London depicts are almost always strong enough to handle the ferocity of the environment into which he places them. Frona Welse of *A Daughter of the Snows* is an overstated and unconvincing example, but many of the other women in the stories say a lot less than she does, and do a lot more. In "The White Silence," Ruth fights off a pack of attacking sled dogs until the Malemute Kid can return. In "The God of His Fathers," Stockard's Indian wife is faithful to the end, and willingly dies with him when they are attacked by the half-breed, Baptiste the Red. And then there is the remarkable Grace Bentham in "The Priestly Prerogative." Grace is burdened with a city-spoiled husband, but she pushes him to buy land at the right time and to move farther north. They become rich, but only because she is strong — the New Woman type London so greatly admired. When men and women figure together in a London story, it is often the woman who is stronger than the man. "And when the short day left them, and the man lay down in the snow and blubbered," London writes concerning Grace's courage and endurance, "it was the woman who lashed him to the sled, bit her lips with the pain of her aching limbs, and helped the dog haul him to Malemute Kid's cabin."

Although the Kid is the main embodiment of survival values in *The Son of the Wolf*, his character and actions are also reflected in Sitka Charley, the Siwash Indian protagonist of several stories. In "The Wisdom of the Trail," Sitka Charley agrees to guide Captain and Mrs. Eppingwell and another white man on "an unknown journey through the dismal vastnesses of the Northland." They are accompanied by two other Indians, Kah-Chucte and Gowhee, whom Charley catches stealing extra rations from the flour sacks. They know that they have contracted to live by the law of the trail, and now they must die by the same law. Charley raises

his rifle and shoots each of the Indians, after first asking how they want to dispose of their possessions.
Sometimes the code makes fierce demands, but Charley lives up to it as faithfully as does the Kid. "Sitka
Charley had achieved the impossible," London writes at
the start of the story. "Other Indians might have known
as much of the wisdom of the trail as did he; but he
alone knew the white man's wisdom, the honor of the
trail, and the law."

London's depiction of Sitka Charley as a man who
is caught between two cultures — that of the Indian and
that of the white man — carries over as a major theme in
Children of the Frost (1902), a collection of stories that
London described to George Brett as an attempt at
showing the Northland experience through the eyes of
the Indian, rather than from the whiteman's point of
view.[6]

London is not entirely accurate in depicting the
differences among the various tribes he writes about,
and sometimes he even fails to distinguish between
Indians and Eskimos, but *Children of the Frost* is nonetheless
effective in its sensitive treatment of native cultures being
haphazardly destroyed by an alien, essentially predatory
one. To London, it seemed inevitable that the aboriginal
tribal system would have little place in the Klondike of the
future, yet he often represents his Indian characters as
being courageous, resourceful, and independent, and he
always is careful to avoid the "noble savage" stereotype.
Many of his Indians possess a code of behavior that is far
superior to the model presented by the white man's lust
for gold. But many of the stories are filled with moods of
dread and revulsion, as if London himself could not quite
bring himself face-to-face with his own characters and the
consequences of their actions, perhaps because of the
many ambivalences he had come to feel about his own
culture in such areas as politics, marriage customs, and
religion. It is sometimes difficult to tell in these stories just

which side London is on. Three of the best examples in this regard are "Keesh, the Son of Keesh," "The League of the Old Men," and "The Law of Life."

Several of London's stories deal with the problems brought on by missionary activity, and in "Keesh" the hero has been taught by Christians that he must not kill. Because of his acceptance of this essential Christian belief, he loses tribal respect and is denied the hand of his betrothed, Su-Su. Unable to endure the taunting that follows him everywhere he goes in the Indian camps, he decides to "go to hell." He murders Su-Su's father and three other men, wraps their severed heads in a moosehide, and carries them to Su-Su's campfire, where he slits her throat. London, in one of his most brutal scenes, shows the impossibility of Keesh's trying to live in two cultures at the same time. In his own way Keesh is trying to live by a new code of manhood, but his actions end in absurdity.

In "The League of the Old Men," the Indians of the Upper Yukon decide to try to halt the encroachment of white culture by killing as many whites as they can, whenever they encounter them on the trail. Imber, the last survivor of the league, finally surrenders in Dawson, where he tells his story as he stands trial. He explains that however unjust it is that the white man can destroy a land that, in his youth, was "warm with sunshine and gladness," he must bend before what seems to him to be a new revelation of cosmic law. London said that this story was his favorite, commenting that "The voices of millions are in the voice of old Imber, and the tears and sorrows of millions are in his throat as he tells his story; his story epitomizes the whole vast tragedy of the contact of the Indian and white man."[7] A point that is often missed concerning "The League of the Old Men" is that the Indians already had the riches and freedom and code of honor that many of the sourdoughs went north to find. Race martyrdom figures in some ways on both sides in this story, and the seeking of gold is perhaps as much a lost cause as is the tragic desire of the Indians to regain lost tribal ways.

These ancient customs involve concepts of justice and decency that have no place in white man's law, however rational they may seem to the Indian. In "The Law of Life," for example, Old Koskoosh is left by his tribe to die in the snow. It is the custom, and he expects it to be carried out. As the wolves close in, he calmly compares himself to an old moose being brought down by the same wolves. Old Koskoosh has learned an essential part of the Law of Life: "Nature was not kindly to the flesh. She had no concern for that concrete thing called the individual. Her interest lay in the species, the race. . . . Nature did not care. To life she set one task, gave one law. To perpetuate was the task of life, its law was death." London's grim view of life is clear enough for us at the end, as Old Koskoosh sits by a dying fire, waiting for bestial but natural forces to put a snarling, tooth-slashing end to his life.

London's interest in the Indians of the Northland is most evident in *Children of the Frost*, but it continues into the later collections of stories as well. In "The Wit of Porportuk," which appears in *Lost Face*, London explores a little-known side of the cultural confrontation in the Klondike: that instead of being destroyed by the new culture, many Indians were able to get rich through various entrepreneurial schemes.

Porportuk, known as the wealthiest Indian in the Yukon, has become a moneylender and a usurer after buying out his partner in a gold strike, the chief Klakee-Nah. Porportuk, although a grandfather, secretly desires Klakee-Nah's young daughter, El-Soo, as his wife. He allows his old friend to borrow money he cannot hope to repay. One evening, while the spendthrift chief is drunk, Porportuk tells him that the debt

can be settled if Klakee-Nah will give him El-Soo. Porportuk is thrown out into the snow by the chief's retain-
ers, but that night the chief dies. Rather than give
herself to Porportuk, El-Soo says she will pay off her
father's debts by auctioning herself to the highest bid-
der, even though she is in love with the young adventurer and hunter, Akoon.

At midnight on Midsummer's Eve, the sky a lurid
red, the auction begins. Porportuk, to his consterna-
tion, gets into a bidding war with an "Eldorado king"
from the Upper Yukon and is forced to go ten thousand
dollars above the actual debt before he wins. El-Soo
pays off what her father actually owed, and throws the
rest of the gold dust into the river. She signs a bill of
sale for herself, and then darts away, pursued by the
outrageously foolish Porportuk amid the jeers and
laughter of the crowd. Twenty-four hours later, Porportuk returns, alone, and hires a gang of trackers to run
El-Soo down. Akoon catches up with her first, however,
and together they flee "across the backbone of the
world."

But their luck does not hold. Akoon is shot in a
hunting accident while they are staying with the Mac-
kenzie Indians, and Porportuk finally finds their camp
and demands El-Soo as his property. After she is brought
over to him, he turns and says he has realized it is no use
for him to try to keep her, because she is like a dog that,
having once run from its master, will surely run again.
He announces that he will thus give her to Akoon, and
has her seated by him. Telling Akoon that he, at least,
will never need to worry about El-Soo running away,
Porportuk quickly crosses her feet and shoots her through
the ankles. The old men of the Mackenzies agree that
justice has been served as the grinning Porportuk departs.

As abruptly hideous as the ending is, "The Wit of
Porportuk" shows once again London's ability to dram-
atize the essential cultural dilemma of his characters.

El-Soo, although a full-blooded Indian, has spent her childhood in a mission school. The nuns want her to complete her education in the United States, but she decides instead to return to her father's house. But this is not exactly a descent into barbarism. "El-Soo drew breath in a cosmopolitan atmosphere," London writes. "She could speak English as well as she could her native tongue, and she sang English songs and ballads. The passing Indian ceremonials she knew, and the perishing traditions. The tribal dress of the daughter of a chief she knew how to wear upon occasion. But for the most part she dressed as white women dress." Like El-Soo, Akoon is also at home in the "cosmopolitan atmosphere" along the Yukon. He had been to Sitka and to the United States, had been to Hudson Bay and back, had sailed as seal-hunter to Siberia and Japan, and had worked as a pilot on the big Yukon steamboats. Even the lovers' nemesis, Porportuk, had earned his fortune the white man's way and is described as "bourgeois." Up to a point, the story is almost comic as London develops the ancient farcical elements implicit in Porportuk's ludicrous pursuit of El-Soo. But when the worst elements in the intermingled cultures come into play — the white man's idea of debt through compound interest, and the Indian's practice of settling scores through the cruel "wit" of savage justice — the story shockingly sets forth the complexities of racial matters in the Northland as London understood them.

London established his lifelong writing habits with his Klondike stories, but his method involved far more than his famous thousand-word-a-day stint. London always said he distrusted the whole idea of inspiration, pointing out that he tried to work slowly, writing in longhand and then revising the day's output when the manuscript was typed. His revisions were seldom extensive, and most of his manuscripts show few changes.

He was not indifferent to style, however, and Frank Norris's pronouncement "Tell your yarn, and let your style go to the devil" has little actual application in London's case. London's style is a distinctive one, but not necessarily a simple one; his best stories, such as "The Wit of Porportuk," constantly build toward points where the writing becomes suddenly elegiac. "I have always insisted that the cardinal literary value is sincerity," London wrote to his publisher in 1907, "and I have striven to live up to this belief."[8]

At the start, at least, London was a careful writer, and he worked hard at mastering his style. "The toil meant nothing to him," he writes in *Martin Eden*. "It was not toil. He was finding speech, and all the beauty and wonder that had been pent for years behind his inarticulate lips was now pouring forth in a wild and virile flood." In dozens of letters to his friends he discussed the way he groped for his own way with language, discussing point of view, suspense, and diction, and stressing how he was determined to hammer his sentences out in sweat and blood. He often claimed to be putting substance above form, but a careful reader of his best work soon realizes this is not so.

As much sudden success as London had with *The Son of the Wolf* and the other Klondike short stories, he wanted to move on to longer forms and convinced S.S. McClure in 1900 to send him a monthly advance of $125 so that he could begin work on *A Daughter of the Snows*. When McClure received the manuscript, he decided not to publish it, and sold the rights to J.B. Lippincott. The book was published in October 1902. London himself regarded the novel as a failure, and fully understood why McClure had balked at bringing it out. "Lord, Lord," London moaned, "how I squandered into it enough stuff for a dozen novels."[9]

Part of the difficulty was that London was working
with Anna Strunsky on *The Kempton-Wace Letters* at the
same time he was writing *A Daughter of the Snows*. But the
main problem was that London tried to turn the book
into a novel of ideas, in which his characters spend
altogether too much time reciting patented formula-
tions of social Darwinism, Nordic supremacy, and most
of the tenets of the wilderness cult. London has his
moments in the novel, especially in his description of
the ordeal of Chilkoot Pass. But the story of how the
timid Vance Corliss becomes a real man by learning
how to smoke, drink, and cuss, thereby winning the
love and respect of Frona Welse, simply will not carry
the load of ideas London wants to pack along.

Frona, the daughter of a Klondike robber baron,
represents London's concept of the New Woman in that
she is "natural, and honest, and true" — all of which
London rather heavily underscores in having her play
Nora in a local production of Henrik Ibsen's *A Doll's
House*. But what is especially significant here is that
London goes several steps beyond Ibsen in having
Frona consciously make a biological choice in selecting
Vance as her husband. She sees him, among the
choices she has, as the best father for her children. It is
not so much that he proves himself worthy of her as that
she selects him to perpetuate her own Anglo-Saxon
stock, "a race of doers and fighters, of globe encirclers
and zone conquerors."

Such ideas have long been cited as examples of
London's excessive biological and racial posturing, and
have sometimes led to the conclusion that he was a
proto-Nazi. But at the time he was writing *A Daughter of
the Snows* there was a great deal of discussion concerning
various methods of improving the human species by
controlling the hereditary factors in mating. The science of eugenics was part of fashionable biology at the
turn of the century, and it was one of London's major

interests. London even wrote a letter to the *Medical Review of Reviews* in 1910 expressing his belief that the human future would be determined by the practice of selective breeding.[10] Although this notion appears to be but one more example of London's obsession with Anglo-Saxon racial superiority, it reveals how central the relationship between animal and human behavior was to his thought and to his fiction. On this score, his ideas now appear to be much more in line with the new hybrid science of sociobiology than they do with the primitive eugenic theories of his era, as can be seen in *The Call of the Wild* and *White Fang*.

London's main reputation as a novelist continues to depend on his two best-known dog books. And his tendency to see himself as part animal — he signed his intimate letters "Wolf," named his mansion "Wolf House," owned a husky called "Brown Wolf," and had a wolf's head as a bookplate — has been interpreted as an all-too-apparent statement of personality by psychologists. London was, however, thoroughly devoted to the ideas of Darwin and Spencer, and this involved more than the idea of the survival of the fittest or his own conception of himself as a predatory beast. Many of his statements about the relationship between humans and animals anticipate those of such recent writers as E.O. Wilson in his 1975 book *Sociobiology: The New Synthesis*. Wilson, regarded as the father of the new science, and other sociobiologists make a case for "the systematic study of the biological basis of all social behavior."[11] Like Wilson, London stresses the importance of applying insights gained from the social behavior of animals (and sometimes even insects) to the study of human nature. London's writings on the subject are more in the spirit of the ethology later popularized by Konrad Lorenz, Robert Ardry, and Desmond Morris, and he knew nothing about the notion of the gene as the unit of evolution, which is what makes sociobiology such a radical departure in the study of animal behavior. Nevertheless, in one prophetic essay, "The Other Animals," published in *Collier's* for September 1908, and included in *Revolution and Other Essays* (1910), London defends himself against a charge of "nature faking" and at the same time sets forth his own understanding of the differences between human and animal thought processes.

The essay, which should be read as a preface to all of London's dog stories, was written in response to President Theodore Roosevelt's attack, in a 1907 interview, on London's depiction of certain episodes in *White Fang* when a bulldog and a lynx both fight a wolf-dog. Roosevelt's specific objections now seem superficial (indeed, he misread the novel on one point), but his concluding remarks reiterated a long-standing criticism of London's accuracy in his Northland stories. "Men who have visited the haunts of the wild beasts, who have seen them, and have learned at least something of their ways," said Roosevelt, "resent such falsifying of nature's records."[12] After pointing out that the President was wrong in the "field observations" he took while reading the book, and stating that whether a "bull-dog can lick a wolf-dog" or not is simply a difference of opinion, London begins his essay by explaining that *The Call of the Wild* and *White Fang* were written partly as a protest against the "humanizing" of animals by other writers.

London flatly states that he believes dogs can indeed think, but that they are "not directed by abstract reasoning, but by instinct, sensation, and emotion, and by simple reasoning." He emphasizes that at all points he has endeavored to keep his work in line with the facts of evolution, and that the idea put forth by the President — that man is the only animal capable of reason — is "distinctly medieval." London agrees that many animal responses are fixed in species through adaptation to environment; however, he objects to the idea that an animal cannot successfully adjust to a strange environment for which heredity has not provided an adjustment. Using observations of "rudimentary reason" in dogs he has owned, he attacks the idea of homocentricity by pointing out that the theory of evolution must include the evolution of reason — a theory that recognizes no impassable gulfs from species to species. "Let us be very humble," London cautions. "We who are so very human are very animal." We cannot deny our "relatives, the other animals," because their history is our history. "What you repudiate in them, you repudiate in yourself — a pretty spectacle, truly, of an exalted animal striving to disown the stuff of life out of which it is made," London writes, "striving by use of the very reason that was developed by evolution to deny the processes of evolution that developed it. This may be good egotism, but it is not good science."

London was not a scientist, of course, and made a number of mistakes in describing animal behavior. He has been criticized most severely for his representation of wolves as savage beasts which inevitably track his characters across the snowfields and gather in a circle around them, waiting for the campfire to go out. Recent studies have shown that wolves are in fact terrified by human beings, and L. David Mech in his book *The Wolf* goes so far as to argue that "In North America, no scientifically acceptable evidence is available to support the claim that healthy wild wolves are dangerous to man."[13] London, along with most who were with him in the Klondike, would have stared in disbelief at anyone who would make such a statement. To be certain, London's concept of the wolf comes out of ancient folklore and superstition that was still very much accepted fact when he was writing. It is true, as Barry Lopez writes in *Of Wolves and Men*, that London's novels "show a preoccupation with 'the brute nature' in men, which he symbolized in the wolf."[14] But London carefully worked out his theories of animal behavior, and he repeatedly pointed out that the dogs and wolves in his stories are not to be taken as literary representations of human types dressed up in fur coats.

London, in his emphasis on "rudimentary reason" and his objection to "humanizing" animals, made a clear distinction between his books and the earlier animal books — Anna Sewell's *Black Beauty* (1877), Rudyard Kipling's *Jungle Book* (1894), and Ernest Thompson Seton's *Wild Animals I Have Known* (1898) — that have sometimes been seen as influences on him. He knew the books, understood the reasons for their popularity, and was trying to capitalize on their success. At the same time, nevertheless, he was presenting a much tougher-minded interpretation of animal behavior and what it can teach us about human nature. Unlike Sewell, London never tries to make us feel sorry for his animals. Unlike Kipling, London never has his animals speak with human voices. And unlike Seton, London does not try to show the essential nobility of animals as an argument for the wilderness-preservation movement.

The term "naturalism" has often been used in reference to London's emphasis on sociological and biological determinism, his belief in the materialistic nature of man, and his reliance on the survival-of-the-fittest thesis; and London is usually classified with Frank Norris and Theodore Dreiser as a "naturalistic" writer. But London's naturalism must be understood in a somewhat different way, in reference to his dog books and his role as a literary precursor of sociobiology. To London, man and animals are similar in most aspects of behavior because all species must live under the Law of Life, which is to say they are all subject to the processes of evolution. Under stress — such as in the Klondike stories — both man and beast must develop methods of survival based on a combination of adaptability and instinct. Some adapt successfully, some revert atavistically, and some perish. But the Law is the same for all, as *The Call of the Wild* and *White Fang* ferociously illustrate.

"Diable, a Dog," which appeared in *Cosmopolitan Magazine* in June 1902 and was reprinted under the title "Bâtard" in *The Faith of Men* (1904), is usually seen as the prototype of *The Call of the Wild.* The story centers on the bond of hatred between Black Leclère and his "devil-dog," Bâtard. Leclère, whose "upper lip had a wolfish way of lifting and showing the cruel white teeth," and Bâtard, whose father was a great gray timber wolf, "acquired a reputation for uncompromising wickedness, the like of which never before attached itself to man and dog."

Leclère works daily on new refinements of his cruelty to Bâtard, one time giving him a permanently drooped ear, another time breaking his ribs. The dog forgets none of this. One day Leclère is falsely convicted of murder. He is taken out, a noose is put around his neck, and he is stood on top of a cracker box. Leclère has agreed that he will leave all of his money to the church if his accusers will hang Bâtard first. But just before the noose is slipped onto the dog, the village storekeeper runs up and yells that the actual murderer has just been brought in at the river landing. Leaving Leclère on the box to meditate on his sins and the ways of providence, the men run off to have a look at the real killer. Bâtard remains with his master. The dog curls his upper lip "almost into a smile," licks his chops, and looks up at Leclère. The dog retreats, faces about, and pauses: "He showed his white teeth in a grin, which Leclère answered; and then hurled his body through the air, in full charge, straight for the box."

Although Buck and White Fang are not the fiendish creatures that Bâtard is, the story does reveal the same "dog psychology" that is behind the characterizations of London's more famous canines. London shows Bâtard "thinking," and writes that just before the dog's fatal charge Leclère "understood what he now had in mind." And earlier, when the dog first approaches the cracker box, London writes that "he came, nearer, the useless ear wabbling, the good ear cocked forward with devilish comprehension." London believed that he was presenting his animal characters in an innovative way, and what he wrote to Brett in 1915 concerning the *Jerry* and *Michael* books applies just as well to the earlier works: "I am making fresh, vivid, new stuff, and dog psychology that will warm the hearts of dog lovers and the heads of psychologists, who usually are severe critics of dog psychology."[15]

The Call of the Wild has sold millions of copies, but Jack London received only $2,700 for it. Seven hundred dollars of the total came from the serialization of the novel in the *Saturday Evening Post*. The remaining two thousand came from George Brett of Macmillan, to whom London sold the book in an outright sale with no royalties possible. This was a decision London said he never regretted. Macmillan agreed to push the novel heavily, and the company more than fulfilled its part of the bargain with deluxe bindings, attractive illustrations, and ambitious promotion. The reviews of *Children of the Frost* and *A Daughter of the Snows* had not been very good, and Brett was taking more of a gamble with London's second novel than is now usually realized. The reviews of *The Call of the Wild* soon told whether the risk had been worth it. "This is by far the best piece of work which has come from the pen of this gifted author," said *Current Literature*. "The book rises above mere story telling and possesses elements of the best in literature — scope, vitality, and fullness."[16] And *The Critic* added: "Buck will live long among the dogs of literature, if, indeed, he does not 'lead the team.'"[17] For the remainder of his career, London was able to demand top dollar for his work, and he said many times that the best deal he ever made was the one with George Brett for two thousand dollars.

The Call of the Wild opens with Buck, half St. Bernard,

half Scotch shepherd, living at Judge Miller's place in "the sun-kissed Santa Clara Valley" in California. Buck is the ruler of his "great demesne," stalking imperiously among the other dogs, "the strange creatures that rarely put nose out of doors or set foot to ground." But in the fall of 1897, "when the Klondike strike dragged men from all the world into the frozen north," Buck is stolen by one of the gardener's helpers, who sells him to pay off a Chinese lottery debt. Buck is valuable property as a potential sled dog, and the price goes up each time he changes owners as he is shipped north. Buck soon learns that "a man with a club was a lawgiver, a master to be obeyed, though not necessarily conciliated." He is bought by two French-Canadians, Perrault and François, who take him and their other dogs on the *Narwhal* to Dyea beach; it is there that Buck is introduced to "the law of club and fang" when he watches Curly, the good-natured Newfoundland, get into a fight with "a husky dog the size of a full-grown wolf." As soon as Curly is knocked down, thirty or forty other huskies close in upon her, "snarling and yelping, and she was buried, screaming with agony, beneath the bristling mass of bodies." François and three men with clubs wade into the mass of dogs and scatter them, but not before Curly is torn to pieces. Buck comes to this conclusion: "So that was the way. No fair play. Once down, that was the end of you. Well, he would see to it that he never went down."

Buck is broken to the traces, learns the secret of burrowing into the snow to find a warm place to sleep, and rapidly adapts to his new environment, even learning how to steal food at every opportunity like the other dogs, proving himself "fit to survive in the hostile Northland environment," as "instincts long dead became alive again." One night Buck, his chief rival Spitz, the rest of the team, and fifty huskies from a nearby camp of the Northwest Police chase a snowshoe hare.

Buck leads the pack, "sounding the old wolf-cry," but Spitz takes a shortcut, intercepts the rabbit, and breaks its back. In a flash Buck is on him, and at the end it is Spitz who goes down to the same snarling fate that Curly had suffered. Buck becomes the new leader of the team, remembering in vague ways "back to the youth of the breed, to the time the wild dogs ranged in packs through the primeval forest and killed their meat as they ran it down. It was no task for him to learn to fight with cut and slash and the quick wolf snap."

Buck and his mates pass from the hands of the two French-Canadians and are acquired by a Scot half-breed to run the "Salt Water Mail" from Dawson to Skagway, where they are again sold, this time to two Americans, Hal and Charles. "Both men were manifestly out of place," comments London, "and why such as they should adventure the North is part of the mystery of things that passes understanding." Accompanying the men is Mercedes, Charles's wife and Hal's sister—"a nice family party." They begin by overloading the sled and tipping it over before they get out of town. They underestimate the amount of dog food needed, and make things worse by overfeeding. The new dogs they had bought to supplement Buck's team die when the rations have to be cut back. Worst of all, Mercedes, who objects every time the men whip the dogs, persists in riding on the sled, adding her own 120 pounds to the already heavy load.

When the dogs stagger into John Thornton's camp at the mouth of the White River, the Arctic spring is well advanced. Thornton warns Hal and Charles that the rotten ice upon which they have been traveling could go at any moment. All the same, they say they will push on to Dawson. Buck, sensing the "impending doom," refuses to get up. Hal lays into Buck with a club until Thornton, "uttering a cry that was inarticulate and more like the cry of an animal," hurls the American backward. Hal draws his long hunting knife, but Thornton raps Hal's knuckles with an ax handle, picks up the knife, and cuts Buck from the traces. A few minutes later, as Thornton kneels beside Buck and searches for broken bones, dog and man watch the sled, the dogs, and the three Americans disappear into the river as a whole section of ice gives way.

Thornton is the "ideal master" who sees to the welfare of his dogs as if they were his own children, talking to them, calling them by love names, and swearing oaths that are love words. In one of his more insightful passages among many describing the communication between men and dogs, London tells us that Buck has his own "love expression" for Thornton. The dog "would often seize Thornton's hand in his mouth and close so fiercely that the flesh bore the impress of his teeth for some time afterward. And as Buck understood the oaths to be love words, so the man understood this feigned bite for a caress."

As soon as the river is clear of ice, Thornton and his two partners, Hans and Pete, break camp and take Buck with them as they float a raft of sawlogs down to Dawson, where they grubstake themselves and set off for the headwaters of the Tanana. Before the year is out, Buck saves Thornton's life twice: once when Thornton gets knocked down in a barroom brawl and another time when Thornton falls into a rapids. But Buck's most memorable feat is when he wins 1,600 dollars on a bet for Thornton and the other two men by pulling a sled loaded with a half-ton of flour from a frozen start on the main street of Dawson.

Thornton is able to pay off all his debts, and he and Pete and Hans, with Buck and a half-dozen other dogs, head "into the East, after a fabled lost mine, the history of which was as old as the country." After two years of wandering, they do not find the mine, but they do discover a shallow placer in a broad valley, "where the gold showed like yellow butter across the bottom of the washing pan." Here they stop, each day earning thousands of dollars in clean dust and nuggets, while the dogs are left on their own. Buck begins ranging deeper and deeper into the forest. He runs with a wolf, he fishes for salmon, he kills a black bear, and the "blood-longing" in him becomes ever stronger. In the fall he pulls down a great bull moose, but when he returns to the camp he finds that Yeehat Indians have slaughtered the three miners and killed the other dogs. The Indians are still dancing about the wreckage of the spruce-bough lodge. Buck hurls himself upon them in "a frenzy to destroy," killing two of them and scattering the rest. "He had killed man, the noblest game of all, and he had killed in the law of club and fang," London writes, paraphrasing Buck's thoughts.

Buck broods in the camp all day. That night a wolf pack streams into the clearing, and Buck, after proving himself by killing one wolf and defending himself against the others, joins the pack. After a few years, the Indians begin to notice a change in the breed of timber wolves; some have markings like Buck, and the Indians begin to talk of a "Ghost Dog" that runs at the head of the pack. Sometimes Indian hunters fail to return, and others are sometimes found in the snow with their throats slashed, enormous wolf prints about them. Each summer Buck returns, alone, to the clearing where Thornton died, "muses for a time," howls once, and departs.

London never wrote better than he did when working on *The Call of the Wild*. "I was unconscious of it at the time," he said in his only explanation of how the novel turned out the way it did. "I did not mean to do it."[18] The book began as just another Klondike story, but London, amazed at himself, acknowledged that it got away from him. Perhaps a passage from the novel itself best accounts for the book's uniqueness:

There is an ecstasy that marks the summit of life, and beyond which life cannot rise. And such is the paradox of living, this ecstasy when one is most alive, and it comes as a complete forgetfulness that one is alive. This ecstasy, this forgetfulness of living, comes to the artist, caught up and out of himself in a sheet of flame.

The enormous attention *The Call of the Wild* brought London is often attributed to its subject. As George Jean Nathan remarked, "In the many years of my incumbency as a magazine editor, it was a general, and occasionally embarrassing fact, that any even half-way good dog story usually attracted wider attention among the readers — and certainly a lot more enthusiastic letters to the editor — than almost anything else."[19]

But *The Call of the Wild* is not just any dog story. London departs from the traditional depictions of dogs in fiction at almost every point. Buck is not cute, he is not gentle, and he does not do clever tricks; at one point he learns to steal, and by the end of the novel he has turned into a killer. Everything he does, he does as London thought a dog actually would. All of his thinking is presented as dog thoughts. And when he begins to respond to his primordial instincts, he does so as a dog, not as a man. It is London's "dog psychology" that contributes the most to the unique effect of the novel and what also makes a lot of critical terminology essentially useless in dealing with it — as well as with much of London's other work. Given the plain, narrative fact that London is showing us a dog as he thinks dogs are, it becomes absurd to refer to Buck as completing "rites of passage" or indulging in "ritualistic acts." This is not to say that *The Call of the Wild* is not an extremely literary novel. The recurring use of the color white, particularly in the scene when Buck and Spitz and the rest of the dogs chase the snowshoe hare, brings *Moby-Dick* to mind. And the relationship between John Thornton and Buck is suggestive of *Huckleberry Finn*. Thornton frees Buck from slavery and learns much about steadfastness and love from him, even though Buck is a "lower" creature, just as Huck learns from Nigger Jim. London's twist, of course, is that it is Buck who lights out for the territory at the end, showing that London, well read as he was, wanted his own way with his own material.

The wonderfully lyric description of Buck's journey with Thornton and his partners in search of the fabled lost gold mine has been interpreted as a "quest" leading to "rites of sacrifice" or "rites of succession" involving totemic animals. But such an approach needlessly complicates the story. In London, atmosphere is sometimes all, and he simply tells us that "In the fall of the year they penetrated a weird lake country, sad and silent, where wild-fowl had been, but where there was no life nor sign of life — only the blowing of chill winds, the forming of ice in sheltered places, and the melancholy rippling of waves on lonely beaches." The imagery alone makes the conclusion of the novel take on its own justification. Thornton and his partners do strike it rich, but the primitive Yeehats kill them, and the even more primitive Buck kills the Indians, thus passing into aboriginal legend as the "Ghost Dog," indeed becoming totemic to the Indians. Still, to London, Buck remains a dog, capable of rudimentary reason but driven by instinct, running "side by side with the wild brother, yelping as he ran." As London warns in his opening sentence, "Buck did not read the newspapers."

Although *White Fang* was written as a companion novel to *The Call of the Wild* and does retain the same techniques in the depiction of animal behavior, it is, to use a metaphor Buck would have appreciated, a far cry from it in narrative quality. London's intention in *White*

Fang, as he explained to George Brett in December of 1904, is to present a "complete antithesis" to *The Call of the Wild* in that it would depict the evolution of domesticity in a dog.[20] But *White Fang*, despite a beautifully detailed opening episode, is flawed from the start. Two men, named Bill and Henry, with a team of six dogs pulling a sled on which is strapped a coffin, are fleeing down a frozen waterway, a wolf pack in pursuit. At night, the dogs are individually lured to their deaths by a she-wolf. Bill goes out with his rifle and three remaining cartridges. Henry hears three shots, but Bill does not return. Henry is left alone to hurl brands from the fire at the encircling wolves. But at the last moment he is rescued as a search party arrives. And that is it. Henry drops out of the novel, and the scene shifts to the wolf pack and the birth of White Fang. It is difficult to understand why either Brett or London allowed the novel to be published as it is. The opening scene is masterfully written, but it is wasted; it does not quite fit, and in that respect it is unfortunately prophetic of much of London's subsequent work.

London's treatment of White Fang's puppyhood, however, is accurately and amusingly written. White Fang, who is three-quarters wolf and one-quarter husky, enters the story in the first month of his life, and London describes his step-by-step development as he emerges from the lair and learns how to hunt. It is apparent at this point in the novel that London had done his research. He read Charles D. Roberts's popular natural history books, *The Kindred of the Wild* (1902) and *Red Fox* (1905), and he checked carefully to find out when wolves mate, how long their period of gestation is, and what time of the year they typically give birth. London even attempts to match White Fang's coloring to his mixed lineage.

Before he is a year old, White Fang is captured by an Indian, Gray Beaver, who trains him as a sled dog, and then takes him to Fort Yukon. Beauty Smith, who is so ugly that his name, as London puts it, was due "to antithesis," is particularly impressed with the dog. Beauty does the cooking, the dishwashing, and the drudgery for the other men in the fort, where he is known for his "cowardly rages" and his "distorted body and twisted mind." But *White Fang* is a novel written partly to demonstrate biological and social determinism, and London insists that although Beauty Smith was "a monstrosity . . . the blame of it lay elsewhere. He was not responsible. The clay of him had been so moulded in the beginning." Beauty Smith has one passion, however; he loves to watch dogfights, and he tries to buy White Fang for that purpose. At first, Gray Beaver refuses, but "Beauty Smith knew the ways of the Indians," and he slyly proceeds to turn Gray Beaver into a drunk. The cook finally buys White Fang for a few bottles of whiskey.

Under Beauty Smith's tutelage White Fang becomes "a fiend," earning a reputation as "The Fighting Wolf," living a public life in a cage. As the sourdoughs crowd around to place their bets, he beats all comers, including a huge mastiff. But he meets his match with a bulldog, who gets a grip on him that White Fang cannot shake. Just as he is to go down for the last time, he is saved by Weedon Scott, who slugs Beauty Smith and manages to free White Fang from the bulldog. Scott, a mining engineer, buys the wolf-dog and takes him back to California.

Weedon Scott's father is Judge Scott, and it is to his estate, Sierra Vista, in the Santa Clara Valley that White Fang is taken. Although mostly wolf by nature, White Fang allows himself to be domesticated, and even allows Weedon's two small children to caress him. But he does this only out of love for his master, and his wild instincts never leave him. One night when an escaped convict named Jim Hall breaks into the house to get the Judge for "railroading" him to prison, White Fang, despite taking three bullets from Hall's revolver, leaps on him and slashes his throat. White Fang lives on to play with his puppies in the California sun. The family from that night on refers to him as "the Blessed Wolf," but he remains what he is — three-quarters wolf — and can never be fully domesticated.

White Fang was published after London's marriage to Charmian, and it reflects London's own decision to tame his appetites, if he could. The reviews were good, and London was properly praised for the novel's greatest strength: its animal side. "Mr. London has fortunately obeyed the call of the wild and returned to the field of his early triumphs," intoned *The Independent*. "This is quite a relief after the mediocre short stories he has been giving us of late. He apparently understands the psychology of brutes, animal and human, better than ordinary tamed and civilized men and women."[21] *The Nation* was more succinct: "As a biographer of wild animals he has hardly an equal."[22]

Like *A Daughter of the Snows*, however, *White Fang* is too deliberately a novel of ideas. The story is structured like an experiment. It is as if London asked himself what would happen if an animal three-quarters wolf and one-quarter dog were suddenly shifted from one environment to another. What does happen is essentially believable, but it is not a very good story. How much more satisfying is the final image of Buck running at the head of the wolf pack than is the final cute picture of White Fang and his puppies. But the main problem is the relentless thesis.

Even though Jim Hall is bent on murdering Judge Scott in his bed, London emphasizes that Hall is not to be blamed for his intention. Hall was "ill-made in the making," London tells us; though Hall is "so terrible a beast that he can best be characterized as carnivorous," it is not his fault. "The more fiercely he fought, the more harshly society handled him, and the only effect of harshness was to make him fiercer," London lectures. "Straight-jackets, starvation, and beatings and clubbings were the wrong treatment for Jim Hall; but it was the treatment he received. It was the treatment he had received from the time he was a little pulpy boy in a San Francisco slum—soft clay in the hands of society and ready to be formed into something." As if this is not enough, we are also told that Hall indeed was wrongfully sent to prison, that the Judge was unwittingly "party to a police conspiracy, that the evidence was hatched and perjured, that Jim Hall was guiltless of the crime charged." Such things can happen, but it is best not to have them happen in fiction. The review that appeared in *The Forum* was, appropriately enough, a slashing one: "It would be an exaggeration to call this novel a Socialistic tract in disguise, but it is not the least clever stroke of its author's that he has succeeded in interweaving into a dog and wolf story so subtle a reminder of the pressure of feral conditions in the midst of civilized human society."[23]

London used the Klondike in a novel for the last time when he wrote *Burning Daylight* (1910). His main enthusiasm in the book is for the later redemptive scenes set on his own Sonoma ranch, but the earlier parts showing Elam Harnish (nicknamed "Burning Daylight") at Circle City and Dawson are the most effective. Even though London is going over old material, his recollections of the Klondike are almost enough to save this otherwise weak novel. It is only when London moves his hero to California that the story line breaks down and Harnish turns into a crankily grotesque version of London himself during his ranching days. Although the novel does not succeed, the opening section is another powerful reminder of what London achieved in his Klondike fiction. As Alfred Kazin points out, "No one before him had discovered the literary possibilities of the Alaskan frontier, and he satisfied the taste of a generation still too close to its own frontier to lack appreciation of 'red-blooded' romance, satisfied it as joyfully and commercially as he knew how."[24]

But for as much as London made out of the Klondike and Alaska as a setting for his fiction, it is surprising to learn that he never returned to Split-Up Island, Dawson, or any of the other places he made famous in his Northland stories and novels. Perhaps the agonies of Chilkoot Pass remained too painful. Perhaps the personal failures in his later life cut him off emotionally from the code of the Northland and his youthful vision of himself as the Malemute Kid. Perhaps it was his own realization that no other scene could evoke the quality of writing that the Northland did, and that for him, as well as for his readers, the land of Arctic gold had become a vast and distant dreamscape, as fragile in its fictional manifestation as Cooper's Adirondacks, Twain's Mississippi, and Melville's South Seas. But perhaps the greatest reason is that in his meditations on man and beast in the Klondike, London reached some conclusions concerning the Law of Life that could only darken with time. As his health failed and his career wound down, the image of Old Koskoosh, the dying fire, and the wolves may have become more vivid to him than those glorious scenes of the Kid on the trail and Buck singing a song of the younger world.

3

~~~~~~

Superman and the Social Pit

Jack London liked to think of himself as a fierce "truth-seeker with a nerve of logic exposed and raw and screaming."[1] However extreme such a conception of his own career might seem, London' s "truth-seeking" did result in the distinctive attitudes that color the intensely meditative and speculative quality of his work. Out of his understanding of elementary Marxism and social Darwinism, he developed a passionate belief in a kind of socialism that was both evolutionary and revolutionary, and he set about illustrating his belief in two powerfully polemic novels, *The Sea-Wolf* and *The Iron Heel*, as well as in several hard-hitting short stories and outspoken essays. London's commitment to his ideas often involved direct personal action as well. He twice ran for mayor of Oakland on the Socialist ticket, getting 245 votes in 1901 and nearly a thousand in 1905. And his devotion to radical politics was not without its personal cost. He angrily acknowledged that he had been "boycotted and blacklisted" on account of his socialism, and he believed that it had cost him hundreds of thousands of dollars in lost royalties.[2] But out of Darwin's dark idea of biological determinism and the survival of the fittest, London was able to extract a shining vision of the ultimate success of the proletariat in the class struggle, a vision that in a surprising way nearly becomes a prophecy of perfectibility.

Although London never made a thoroughly systematic statement of his ideas and never fully worked out a satisfactory reconciliation between his own rampant individualism and the egalitarianism implicit in socialist theory, his philosophy of life continued to evolve right down to his last days. He has often been interpreted as a specialist in despair, who made his characters out to be raging beasts or suicides and whose impulses took him to the very edge of fascism. There are indeed several negative aspects to London's thoughts, and his repeated emphasis on Anglo-Saxon racial supremacy is certainly the most infamous example. Nevertheless, his writing constantly demonstrates his recognition that the world is painfully full of cruelty and that it is the duty of the strong to help the weak develop strengths of their own. He saw himself preaching a "gospel of service," and wrote, in his moving introduction to Upton Sinclair's 1915 anthology *The Cry for Justice*, that "this fair world so brutally unfair, is not decreed by the will of God nor by any iron law of Nature." London went on to say we should "learn that the world can be fashioned a fair world indeed by the humans who inhabit it, by the very simple, and yet most difficult process of coming to an understanding of the world."[3]

London's own understanding of the world has its origins in the hundreds of books he read, especially during his great period of self-education after he returned to Oakland from the Erie County Penitentiary in 1894. He was greatly influenced, as noted, by Darwin, Spencer, Nietzsche, and Marx, but not in as direct and rigid a way as is sometimes assumed. London read widely and rapidly, picked up many of his key ideas secondhand, and had no reservations about appropriating useful concepts wherever he could find them. Among the many books that directly influenced him are two by a now obscure but once enormously important writer: Benjamin Kidd, the British popularizer of the philosophy of Herbert Spencer and author of

Social Evolution (1894) and *Principles of Western Civilization* (1902). Joan London was one of the first to point out London's dependence on Kidd, and it is now apparent that London not only read him but made considerable use of his key terms and ideas.[4]

Like London, Kidd had fallen under the influence of Spencer. But with his energetic, lucid style, Kidd was able to soften some of Spencer's harsh Darwinism. Kidd combined Spencer's emphasis on the survival of the fittest with the principle of natural selection and came up with a theory "that the mass of men must consent, in the interests of progress, to yield to the few superior individuals who will be selected to rule society and to keep it at the maximum of efficiency."[5]

In outlining his program for attaining such a society, Kidd suggested first of all that group restraint, based on Christian ethics, would work to curb individual selfishness. Using examples from history, he saw an evolutionary movement in that direction, but only in Western civilization, particularly in its Anglo-Saxon phase, which had been the most deeply affected by "altruistic influences." Describing a destiny that would work itself out through the law of natural selection, Kidd argued that the weaker races would simply disappear through contact with the stronger ones. Subsequent events, such as World War I and the rise of fascism, discredited Kidd's philosophy, but his ideas were very much a part of the intellectual and political climate when London read him. And as negative as Kidd's conviction of racial destiny may have been, as far as London's thought was concerned, it must be remembered that London grew up at a time when most Americans of original British stock, as he thought himself to be, believed they were naturally superior to their immigrant neighbors. In addition, London lived in California at a time when state legislatures on the West Coast were busily passing discriminatory legislation against the Chinese and the Japanese.

At first it might appear that Kidd's influence could have little bearing on London's socialism, but London identified socialist theories with ethnologically Anglo-Saxon ideals and traditions. In explaining his position to Cloudesley Johns in 1899, London cautioned him to understand that while we are under the control of "great unreasoning forces," these forces, through "merciless natural law," nonetheless "generated the altruistic in man," and that only the race with the highest degree of altruism will survive: "The lesser breeds cannot endure."[6] London saw himself as a "scientific socialist," because he firmly believed that socialism had its basis in both natural selection and the Malthusian doctrine that the population of the world tends to increase faster than the food supply, and that war, famine, and disease are inevitable natural restrictions on population.

Although when caught up in his enthusiasm for socialist causes he could refer to his "comrades world-wide," London did not have much faith in the universal brotherhood of man. "Socialism is not an ideal system, devised by man for the happiness of all life; nor for the happiness of all men; but it is devised for the happiness of certain kindred races," he said in 1900 in one of the best explanations of his position.[7] London stressed that because of the "logic of events," the mass of men must be ruled by the few, and that socialism, which will evolve naturally out of the Anglo-Saxon tradition of democracy, will provide the best conditions for furthering a just society based on the highest principle of unselfish concern for the welfare of others. At his moments of greatest affirmation in his writing and lecturing, this is the socialist vision London projects. At other times, of course, it is a different story, and he found much in Kidd that simply served to rationalize race prejudice. London sometimes used the idea of altruism to justify his own money-grubbing, explaining that much of what he made was donated to revolutionary purposes, and that he was merely beating the capitalists at their own game in his conception of himself as both literary businessman and rancher. Just because he believed that socialism would eventually triumph did not mean that he could turn his back on the tooth-and-nail world he would have to survive in as long as capitalism remained dominant.

London's eventual disillusionment with the Socialist Party and his resignation from it were prompted by his fear that the leadership had become weak and divided, and that it had lost its "fire and fight." In his resignation letter, London stressed that races and classes must gain freedom through their own "strength of brain and brawn."[8] London's emphasis in the same letter on revolution through strength, of the need for "superior individuals" to lead and inspire the masses to "wrest" liberty and freedom from the capitalists underscores the influence of Friedrich Nietzsche on his conception of revolutionary socialism. Like the vast majority of Nietzsche enthusiasts at the turn of the century, London probably did not read any of the German philosopher's books from beginning to end — with the possible exception of Nietzsche's most famous, *Thus Spake Zarathustra* (1884), which was available in English translation by 1900. Nietzsche, with the iconoclasm implicit in his most memorable aphorisms — such as "God is dead!" — came across at times like a vengeful saboteur of bourgeois values, and he had automatic appeal to London and other young socialists, however ignorant they were of the many contradictions in his thought. *The Nation* remarked on Nietzsche's reputation by suggesting, in 1913, "that nowhere will you find more men who regard Nietzsche favorably or tolerantly than among those Socialistically inclined; they feel and welcome the destructive energy of the man, while caring little that his programme of construction is entirely opposed to their own."[9] But London found that Nietzsche's

ideas meshed quite well with his own, and he applied
them to his own peculiar amalgam of evolutionary socialism and Anglo-Saxon racial superiority.

Darwinism, as London and most of his contemporaries interpreted it, was seen as a reductionist biological philosophy: the attempt to explain all life, and perhaps the class struggle itself, in terms of a single
principle. Nietzsche had a similar line of thought, but
for him all human behavior could be reduced to a single basic drive, the will to power. Man wants to perfect
himself, to reach a more powerful state of being, to
become a creator rather than a mere creature. Most fail
in this pursuit and choose to seek crude, abusive power
over others as a substitute. But there is another type of
man, the superman — perhaps better translated from
Übermensch as "overman" — who has overcome *himself*, a
higher type who is the master of his own passions and
who can actually employ his will to power creatively
instead of vulgarly. Nietzsche posits the idea of the
superman as a challenge, not a certainty, and he did
not believe that either biological or social evolution
would produce a race of supermen, much less one superman. Indeed, Nietzsche dismissed faith in progress
as merely a modern idea, and a false one at that. London, however, with his personal emphasis on strength,
virility, and sheer genius, seized on the idea of the
superman and explored it in contrasting ways in *The
Sea-Wolf* and *The Iron Heel*. The first novel, with its depiction of Wolf Larsen and his failure to understand the
will to power within a socialist context, is an attack on
the popular misconception of Nietzsche's idea of the
superman. The second, with its depiction of Ernest
Everhard and his successful use of his improved self as
a spokesman for socialism, represents London's positive adaptation of Nietzsche's ideas.

Numerous prejudices have resulted from London's
willingness to combine his own ideas with those of oth-

er writers, particularly with those of Nietzsche. It did
not help that during the Hitler years the Nazis published several misleading and seriously expurgated
anthologies of Nietzsche's work. Although Nietzsche's
name appears in the first sentence of *The Sea-Wolf*—the
scholar and dilettante Humphrey Van Weyden is on his
way to visit a friend who loafs through the winter
months reading Nietzsche and Schopenhauer "to rest
his brain"—London later was careful to point out that
the superman concept in the book is not the one he
endorsed. And he even claimed, in a 1915 letter to
Mary Austin, a member of the Artist and Writer's Colony of Carmel, that *The Sea-Wolf* was actually an attack
on Nietzsche and his superman idea.[10] London's image
as a lone-wolf adventurer led his audience to associate
him too readily with Wolf Larsen, whose own "little
world"—the ship over which he brutally and egotistical-
ly presides in his "infinite ambition and infinite loneli-
ness"—is the very image of the slave society Jack London the socialist wanted to reform through fiery
revolution. But as much as London lamented the mis-
reading of *The Sea-Wolf*, he must have realized that his
own success in creating Wolf Larsen as a brooding Lucifer, a raging Captain Ahab, a melancholy Hamlet,
and a kind of saltwater Faust tended to obscure the
novel's thematic purposes.

Larsen, "a magnificent atavism," with eyes as
"bleak, and cold, and grey as the sea itself," fishes the
unfortunate Van Weyden from San Francisco Bay after
a ferry collision, and takes him aboard the *Ghost*, an
eighty-ton schooner bound seal hunting to Japan. Larsen refuses to return Van Weyden to San Francisco or
to transfer him to another ship. Instead, he forces him
to sign on as cabin boy at twenty dollars a month,
nicknames him "Hump," and puts him to work setting
tables, peeling potatoes, and washing dishes for the
ship's crew of seal hunters, who argue, roar, and curse
"like some semi-amphibious breed." Van Weyden is

forced to be their slave from half-past five in the morning till ten o'clock at night. But when he goes to clean Larsen's stateroom for the first time, he discovers a rack filled with volumes of Shakespeare, Poe, and Tennyson, as well as scientific works by Tyndal and Darwin, along with books on astronomy and physics. Between the blankets on the bunk is the Cambridge Edition of Browning, with passages underlined in pencil. Larsen, whom Van Weyden describes as "a man so purely primitive that he was of the type that came into the world before the development of the moral nature," suddenly becomes more enigmatic than atavistic.

During their first conversation, when Van Weyden goes to Larsen to complain about the cook, the captain sneers at Van Weyden and abruptly asks him if he believes in the immortal soul. This is the first of a series of discussions that loosely structure what London later referred to as "the black philosophy that I worked out at that time and afterwards put into Wolf Larsen's mouth."[11] Larsen barely waits for Van Weyden's hesitant answer to the question before he responds with a pure statement of the bleak materialism his reading has confirmed. Larsen says that life is "like yeast, a ferment, a thing that moves and may move for a minute, an hour, a year, or a hundred years, but that in the end will cease to move. The big eat the little that they may continue to move, the strong eat the weak that they may retain their strength. The lucky eat the most and move the longest, that is all."

As the novel continues, Van Weyden and Larsen at various times discuss Browning, Herbert Spencer, the Bible (Ecclesiastes is Larsen's favorite book), and Shakespeare (*Hamlet* is his favorite play), and everywhere Larsen finds confirmation of his pessimism, which he is more than willing to put into action. One of the boatmen tells Van Weyden that Larsen is a "regular devil" and the *Ghost* a "hell-ship." Two years earlier, Larsen had shot four of his own crew to settle an argument and, not long after, he had killed a man with a single blow of a fist, smashing the man's head like an eggshell. "The earth is as full of brutality as the sea is full of motion," Larsen says in talking to Van Weyden about "the value of life." Larsen tells him that "life is the cheapest thing in the world," that it has no value other than what it puts upon itself, and that "Nature spills it out with a lavish hand. Where there is room for one life, she sows a thousand lives, and it's life eat life till the strongest and most piggish life is left."

Van Weyden has plenty of opportunity, when the ship catches the northeast trade winds, to observe how Larsen toys with the minds of his men, probing them "with the cruel hand of a vivisectionist, groping about in their mental processes and examining their souls as though to see of what soul-stuff is made." More and more, Van Weyden learns that Larsen has become a man "utterly without morals" and is to be feared "like a snake, or a tiger, or a shark." It therefore makes Van Weyden nervous when, after he explains a Browning poem to Larsen, the captain frees him of his duties and has him discuss "life, literature, and the universe" for three days. Van Weyden is warned by the crew to look out for squalls, and at the end of the third day one hits. Larsen loses his temper when Van Weyden gets too bold in his comments, and grabs him by the arm with such a powerful grip that Van Weyden collapses onto the floor. Another time, Larsen ends one of their discussions in an even more forceful way when he demonstrates a thesis — that the instinct of life is stronger than the instinct of immortality — by nearly choking Van Weyden to death.

But the captain continues to display an oddly confessional friendship to Van Weyden. Larsen demonstrates a navigational tool he has invented, tells him about his childhood on Norwegian coastal ships, and recounts his early attempts at educating himself while in the English merchant service. At the end of his history, Larsen says that only "Death" Larsen, his brother and master of the sealing steamer *Macedonia*, knows more about him than does Van Weyden. Death Larsen, as Van Weyden learns, is widely suspected of opium smuggling, slave trading, and open piracy. As one of the crew says, the two brothers "hate one another like the wolf-whelps they are."

The *Ghost* sails on amid "a carnival of brutality," while Larsen begins to suffer increasingly from strange headaches so fierce that one day Van Weyden finds him in his stateroom sobbing convulsively, his head buried in his hands. The crew moves toward mutiny, but the still-powerful Larsen fights his way out when attacked by a half-dozen men in the darkness of the forecastle. After Van Weyden tends to Larsen's wounds, the captain promotes him to mate and increases his pay to seventy-five dollars a month. In an echo of Kipling's *Captains Courageous* (1897) and Frank Norris's *Moran of the Lady Letty* (1898), novels in which greenhorns develop into capable sailors, Van Weyden thrives under his new responsibilities, and says, "I grew to love the heave and roll of the *Ghost* under my feet as she wallowed north and west through the tropic sea."

The ship proceeds north to the Bering Sea, where the migrating seal herd is finally sighted and the harvest can begin, the crew "ravaging and destroying, flinging the naked carcasses to the shark and salting down the skins so that they might later adorn the fair shoulders of the women of the cities." The decks become slippery with fat and blood, and the scuppers run red. Van Weyden realizes that he has been changed for good, that Larsen has opened up for him "the world of the real."

While cruising about, the *Ghost* runs across an open boat containing four men and a woman who were on a mail steamer bound for Yokohama when the ship sank in a typhoon. The woman is Maud Brewster, a poet and essayist, and, from the moment she is taken aboard the *Ghost*, the old superstition about a woman passenger jinxing a whaling or sealing ship certainly comes true as far as the narrative is concerned. Interest in Wolf Larsen as a demonic philosopher diminishes as the once terse dialogue between Larsen and Van Weyden turns into a stilted discussion of literary matters with Maud at the center. This is not to say that Larsen's behavior changes, however. Maud soon has a chance to get her own introduction to Larsen's cruelty in action as he orders the cook to be keelhauled for failing to keep the galley clean. "Like a fresh-caught fish on a line," the cook is pulled back aboard, his right foot amputated by a shark. Instead of tending to the cook, Larsen throws out a hook baited with salt pork, catches the shark, props its mouth open with a sharpened stake, and then returns the creature to the sea, where it will die a lingering death of starvation. The madness continues when the *Ghost* meets the *Macedonia* and Larsen orders his hunters to open fire on his brother's boats.

That night, Van Weyden awakens to a feeling of danger and discovers Larsen trying to rape Maud. When Van Weyden strikes him, Larsen flings him across the stateroom. Van Weyden draws his sheath knife, but then Larsen begins to stagger back and forth, suddenly stricken with one of his debilitating headaches. When Larsen collapses into his bunk, Van Weyden and Maud see their chance to escape. Provisioning one of the ship's boats, the two sail for Japan. After days and nights of storm, they land on a damp and rocky seal rookery they name Endeavor Island. To satisfy his nervous editors — who objected to an unmarried couple marooned by themselves — London has Van Weyden and Maud build separate huts out of driftwood. It is this scene that most distressed Ambrose Bierce and other critics who otherwise admired the novel for London's "hewing out and setting up" of "that tremendous creation Wolf Larsen." As Bierce complained, "The love element, with its absurd suppressions and impossible proprieties, is awful. I confess to an overwhelming contempt for both the sexless lovers."[12]

Their chaste solitude ends, however, when Wolf Larsen is once more brought into the narrative. The *Ghost*, her masts fallen, drifts ashore on Endeavor Island with only one person aboard, Larsen himself, who explains that his brother finally caught up with him, persuaded the crew to desert, and left him adrift on his own ship. Now blind, his headaches intensifying by the hour, Larsen remains aboard the grounded ship. Incredibly, Van Weyden and Maud manage to re-step the masts. They devise a hoisting tackle, hook it to the ship's windlass, and crank the fallen timbers into place. To protect their work, they handcuff Larsen hand and foot. He suffers a stroke and is paralyzed on his right side. He begins to lose his voice, and as he starts to slip toward death Maud asks him his thoughts on immortality. The last word he is able to utter is "B-O-S-H." They bury him at sea, Maud whispering, "Good-by, Lucifer, proud spirit." The novel ends with Maud and Van Weyden being picked up by a United States revenue cutter. They look into each other's eyes and say "My woman" and "My man."

The Sea-Wolf was one of London's most financially successful works, and it was, in most respects, the perfect book to follow *The Call of the Wild*. Despite the narrative breakdown when Maud Brewster enters the story and the disturbingly insipid ending, the novel is literally stuffed with powerful literary ingredients. London once more drew upon the romance of his past for the essential details, basing most of the actual sailing scenes on his trip to the Bonin Islands and the Bering Sea aboard the *Sophie Sutherland* in 1893. His original plan was to freshen his memory by engaging cabin passage in a sailing vessel and actually writing the novel while at sea. The plan did not work out, but London's ability to evoke psychological terror through portentous imagery nonetheless gives *The Sea-Wolf* a menacingly authentic atmosphere. The fog, for instance, is

like the gray shadow of infinite mystery, brooding over the whirling speck of earth; and men, mere motes of light and sparkle, cursed with an insane relish for work, riding their steeds of wood and steel through the heart of the mystery, groping their way blindly through the Unseen, and clamoring and clanging in confident speech the while their hearts are heavy with incertitude and fear.

The ship itself becomes a hellish world dominated by the devil himself: Wolf Larsen is not only referred to as "Lucifer" at the end, he likes to discuss the meaning of *Paradise Lost* with Van Weyden. During most of the voyage, the weather is ominous, constantly reminding the reader of impending disaster as the *Ghost* sails toward an "eastern sky filled with clouds that overpowered us with some black sierra of the infernal regions." But it is the presence of Wolf Larsen that contributes the most to the nightmarishly Gothic qualities of the novel.

Able to squeeze a raw potato to a pulp, yet increasingly weakened by some terrible agony within his skull, Larsen is a composite figure embodying elements drawn from a catalog of literature's legendary losers. Through a series of unsubtle allusions, London associates him with Shakespeare's Hamlet, Milton's Satan, Goethe's Faust, Browning's Caliban, and Melville's Captain Ahab. But Larsen differs from all of these tragic heroes in that his tragedy seems ultimately to be without purpose. He is Ahab without a white whale to pursue, a Satan who does not believe in God. He is a Hamlet without a murder to avenge, a Faust who does not believe it is possible to transcend human limitations. And he is a Caliban who seeks to overcome his own beastliness by trying to understand the refinements of poetry. The nihilism implicit in his materialism makes him into a prototype of the twentieth-century anti-hero, doomed to extinction because he alienates himself from others through his own intellectual rebelliousness.

Most of all, Larsen is London's version of the failed superman, who turns his instinctive will to power into mere selfishness — as he demonstrates when he plays cards with the drunken cook and wins $185 that the cook had stolen from Van Weyden. When Hump asks for his money back, Larsen gives him a lesson in ethics, saying that "Might is right, and that is all there is to it. Weakness is wrong." Larsen goes on to discuss the idea shared by Spencer and Kidd that altruism is imperative to the ideal of highest conduct. Larsen says that he has his own version of their dictum that the altruistic man should act first for his own benefit, next for the benefit of his children, and third for the benefit of the race; Larsen prefers to simplify the matter by cutting out the children and the race. "But with nothing eternal before me but death," he muses, "given for a brief spell this yeasty crawling and squirming which is called life, why, it would be immoral for me to perform any act that was a sacrifice." As London told Charmian regarding the novel's underlying psychological motif, "The superman is anti-social in his tendencies, and in these days of our complex society and sociology he cannot be successful in his hostile aloofness. Hence the unpopularity of the financial supermen like Rockefeller; he acts like an irritant in the social body."[13] Larsen fails to realize that because he cannot cooperate with others and cannot conceive of self-sacrifice, his great strength is ultimately wasted. His aloofness is biologically unnatural because it denies the social virtues that make human survival possible.

Larsen, for all his creativeness and power, lacks

adaptability; it is Van Weyden who possesses the true potential for survival. Larsen is on a wandering course that takes him ever closer to his fatal meeting with his brother, Death. Van Weyden, on the other hand, is saved from drowning at the start of the novel, and then steadily gains strength and resourcefulness until he proves himself as a real man in a man's world, showing that he is worthy of Maud's love. Larsen, with his savage pessimism, lives in an "unnatural and unhealthful" environment, and can only conceive of love as a form of rape. His lust for life is a blind lust, and at the end he loses both his sight and his ability to speak. Able to remember only one part of the burial service, Van Weyden can only say, "And the body shall be cast into the sea," as he lifts the hatch cover on the *Ghost* and Larsen's canvas-shrouded corpse slips overboard and is dragged down to the depths by a weight of iron. Van Weyden, however, after having played something of a seagoing Adam to Maud's Eve, lives to be rescued, significantly, by a revenue cutter that is presumably on patrol to catch the likes of Wolf Larsen, a man who believed in neither taxes nor duties. In this respect, Larsen takes on another dimension, coming to represent the inefficient, brutal, wasteful, and undemocratic capitalism that London attacks more directly and more viciously in *The Iron Heel*.

One of the most apocalyptic novels of this century, *The Iron Heel* is London's most direct, most sustained attack on capitalism. London's protagonist, the socialist intellectual Ernest Everhard, who represents the altruistic superman that Wolf Larsen fails to become, flatly tells an audience of investors, industrialists, and financiers that "you have failed in your management of society, and your management is to be taken away from you." The novel is in the form of the "Everhard Manuscript," written by Everhard's widow, and covers the

years 1912–1932, when her husband battles the capitalist Oligarchy, or "Iron Heel," that establishes absolute control over the American government. The manuscript turns up seven centuries later, at a time when
Everhard and his cause have finally been vindicated.
The historian Anthony Meredith edits the manuscript
and provides a running commentary on the narrative
through dozens of footnotes.

Everhard is one of London's self-projections, the
revolutionist he would have liked to be if he could have
overcome his obsession with money and property.
Everhard is built like a boxer, but he is so skilled in
argument that he easily crushes all of the businessmen,
professors, and lawyers who dare to challenge his opinions. Unfortunately for the story line, he wins his debates too easily, and too much of the novel is given over
to tedious lectures in which he relentlessly expounds
the socialist case against capitalism. Everhard's insis-
tence that the revolution could never succeed through
the ballot box alone, and that the day will come when
the capitalists must be answered "in roar of shell and
shrapnel and in whine of machine guns," prompted
many of London's fellow socialists to object to the kind
of dangerous prophecy that could only hurt the recruit-
ment of party members.

The Iron Heel had its genesis in London's reading of
W.J. Ghent's *Our Benevolent Feudalism* (1902), a book that
predicted the emergence of "a renascent feudalism" as
the power of capital over labor increased. Ghent argued
that a gigantic merger of industries would lead to a
benevolent despotism that would bind labor to the ma-
chines in the same way that serfs were once bound to
the soil. London reviewed the book in the *International
Socialist* and warned about assuming that the capitalists
were unable to prevent the eventual triumph of socialism. London held the Marxist idea that society would
inevitably split into just two classes, and that capitalist

and proletarian would have to slug it out in a final
Armageddon. By the time he began working on *The
Iron Heel*, however, he had begun to question the
progress of the coming revolution. And in the novel he
confronts the possibility that socialism might not succeed at all, that the party leaders had underestimated
the strength of their adversaries and that in a hard-
fought struggle capitalism might prevail. The book was
thus intended as a warning to the smug, pacifist socialists he thought were undermining their own cause.[14]

The novel also had its origins in London's lecture
tour of 1906. While in New York during the early part
of January, he was asked to speak to an audience of the
very rich. Just as he has Everhard do in *The Iron Heel*,
London conducted a vicious frontal attack on the sensi-
bilities of his listeners, telling them that seven million
socialist revolutionaries were going to strip them of everything they owned. "London walked down from the
rostrum through a sea of blasted, purple faces distorted
with rage, but no attempt was made to restrain him,"
recalled one observer. "It was not until he was well out
of earshot that some of the stunned audience plucked
up enough courage to remark that 'he ought to be in
jail.'"[15]

In many respects London took some serious professional risks with *The Iron Heel*. He set forth strong
opinions on a dangerous topic, and in his attack on
both the "pig-ethics" of capitalism and the overconfi-
dence of the socialists, he invited (and got) bad reviews
from all sides. London looked upon the book as a labor
of love, but the book-buying public did not want to
have much to do with it. Not until many years later
would political events contribute to the novel's reputation as one of the most revolutionary texts ever written
by an American.

London had long been bothered by a naive assumption on the part of his socialist comrades that the

capitalists would quietly step aside and allow the socialists to take control of industry simply on the basis of a
workers' majority at the polls. He did not believe that
the magnates of business and industry would stand by
and let themselves be voted out of existence, and in an
early essay, "The Question of the Maximum," included
in *War of the Classes*, he cautioned that the ruling class,
when threatened with a revolution, would place "a
strong curb . . . upon the masses until the crisis was
past." After the Russian revolution of 1905 ended in the
violent suppression of the workers, he became even
more convinced that American socialists had failed to
take into account that the capitalist class would strike
back, and strike back hard. London did not want to
deny the necessary evolutionary triumph of socialism;
he did stress, however, that the fight would be a long
one, and that the first consequence could well be a
terrible defeat leading to the establishment of a capitalist dictatorship more brutal than any in history. This is
precisely what *The Iron Heel* predicts.

"A superman, a blond beast such as Nietzsche
described," Ernest Everhard makes his appearance in
the first few pages of the novel by using his "smashing,
sledge-hammer manner of attack" to tell off the other
guests at a polite dinner party being given by John
Cunningham, a University of California physics professor. Everhard bulls his way into a discussion of the
responsibility of the churches concerning the plight of
oppressed labor, tells several of the ministers involved
in the debate that their sociology is "vicious and worth-
less," and convinces them that their method of thinking
is utterly wrong.

This manner of approach, as eloquent as Everhard
usually is, soon becomes boorish, despite Avis Everhard's worshipful tone. George Orwell provided an appropriate criticism in pointing out that "the kind of
book which consists of conversations where the person

the author agrees with has the best of it is quite obviously a way of revenging the conversational defeats which one suffers in real life."[16] In his all-knowing certitude, Everhard becomes an increasingly grotesque spokesman for London's opinions. But he succeeds in making a big impression on Avis, who is Professor Cunningham's daughter. Everhard, who has written a book entitled *Working-class Philosophy*, soon shows Avis "a new and awful revelation of life." In her gushing style, she testifies that Everhard reveals himself to her as "the apostle of truth, with shining brows and the fearlessness of one of God's own angels, battling for the truth and the right, and battling for the succor of the poor and lonely, and oppressed." Her last doubts concerning her love for him vanish when she hears him lecture to the Philomath Club, a select organization of the wealthiest people on the Pacific Coast.

Speaking of his birth in the working class, tracing his boyhood in the mills, mentioning how he learned the horse-shoeing trade, and recounting his struggle for an education, Everhard explains how his involvement with the socialist movement brought him into touch with "all the splendid, stinging things of the spirit." The audience listens appreciatively until he begins to talk about the twenty-five million socialists worldwide and how they will form an "army of revolution" to take what is rightfully theirs. "A low throaty rumble arose, lingered on the air a moment and ceased," Avis relates. "It was the forerunner of the snarl, and I was to hear it many times that night—the token of the brute in man, the earnest of his primitive passions." Everhard concludes with the same two sentences London used at the end of his lectures: "This is the revolution, my masters. Stop it if you can." A dozen men want to argue with him, but he coolly dispenses with them individually. At the end of the debate, one of the industrialists finally rises and states what his side is prepared to do if the working class ever does come out on top on election day: "We will grind you revolutionists down under our heel, and we shall walk upon your faces. The world is ours, we are its lords, and ours it shall remain." If that is to be the case, replies Everhard, the workers will answer with bullets: "Power will be the arbiter, as it always has been the arbiter. It is a struggle of classes. Just as your class dragged down the old feudal nobility, so shall it be dragged down by my class, the working class. If you will read your biology and your sociology as clearly as you do your history, you will see that this end is inevitable."

Everhard follows this speech a few days later with another one, this time to a group of farmers and owners of small businesses. He tells them that their only hope is to ally themselves with the socialists. Only by taking over the capitalist trusts and running them for the benefit of all people can there be a just society. He also lectures them on the hidden flaw built into the capitalist system. Referring to the Marxist theory of surplus value, he says that because capitalists refuse to pay workers sufficient wages to consume the goods that are produced, all industrial nations will eventually pile up a surplus beyond what they can hope to export. Rather than raise the pay of workers so that they can buy the goods, the capitalists will throw the merchandise into the sea. Everhard warns his audience that if they do not wake up and realize that the middle class is doomed to suffer as much as the workers under this system of overproduction and artificially high prices, they "will be crushed under the iron heel of a despotism as relentless and terrible as any despotism that has blackened the pages of the history of man."

Ironically, it is the capitalists who are awakened by Everhard's lectures. An Oligarchy, consisting of a small committee of the major captains of industry, is formed. Patriotic vigilante gangs are given free rein to smash

socialist presses and disrupt meetings. The army is
brought in to break up strikes. And the papers, the
schools, and the churches do nothing as the Oligarchy
pursues its goals. Everhard's associates continue to believe in democratic processes, and still pin their hopes
on the ballot box. But even after they elect him to
congress, Everhard insists that ballots are not enough.
The socialist movement does achieve a great victory
when a general strike of workers in Germany and the
United States prevents a war between the two nations
over competition for export markets. But the success is
momentary. The Oligarchy institutes the "Mercenar-
ies," professional soldiers who slaughter revolutionists.
Labor leaders are rounded up on false indictments.
And fifty socialist congressmen are arrested on a phony
charge of exploding a bomb while the House of Repre-
sentatives is in session. A workers' Commune is established in Chicago, but the Oligarchy is willing to destroy the city to crush the movement. This part of the
novel, with its horrifyingly graphic descriptions of civil
war, constitutes some of London's most powerful writing. But the Commune falls as the Oligarchy establishes a Russian passport system, sets up elaborate systems
of surveillance, and goes about "punishing without
mercy and without malice, suffering in silence all retal-
iations that were made upon it, and filling in the gaps
in its fighting line as fast as they appeared."

For Everhard, however, the fight is far from over.
He escapes from prison and makes his way to California, where Avis and his surviving comrades have prepared a refuge in Sonoma County. From this base they
promote terrorism against the Oligarchy and plan for
the Second Revolt. Everhard dies a martyr when he is
captured and executed in 1932. But his prophecy holds
true: "Tomorrow the cause will rise once more, stronger
in wisdom, and in discipline." Just before Avis is appre-
hended, she hides the manuscript in a hollow oak at

Wake Robin Lodge. "Little did she realize," the editor
writes, "that the tortuous and distorted evolution of the
next three centuries would compel a Third Revolt and a
Fourth Revolt, and many Revolts, all drowned in seas
of blood, ere the world movement of labor should come
into its own."

In an interview with a socialist reporter several
years after *The Iron Heel* came out, London reiterated
the novel's central point: "History shows that no master
class is ever willing to let go without a quarrel. The
capitalists own the governments, the armies, and the
militia. Don't you think the capitalists will use these
institutions to keep themselves in power? I do."[17] This
message, not Everhard's socialist preachments, is what
gave the novel its later relevance. "We have but to substitute the word 'fascism' for 'oligarchy' and *The Iron Heel*
becomes a living picture of what actually happened in
the past two decades," Philip S. Foner wrote in 1947.[18]

The Iron Heel is a product of London's years of
greatest involvement with the socialist cause, although
London's actual contributions to leftist political movements, as well as the very nature of his socialist ideology, remain matters of considerable controversy. London obviously got a far different reading out of *The
Communist Manifesto* than did most of his socialist contemporaries, who were more interested in promoting
municipal reforms through legitimate political means
than they were through the whine of machine-gun bullets and shrapnel. London's call for the outright destruction of "bourgeois society with most of its sweet
ideals and dear moralities" in such essays as "Revolution" (*Contemporary Review*, January 1908, reprinted in
Revolution and Other Essays) made him a hero among the
Russian proletariat, and the writers Maxim Gorky and
Leonid Andreyev were among his major enthusiasts.
This was especially the case after London gave a speech
in Boston in 1905 proclaiming the "Russian Nihilist

assassins" his comrades, adding: "There are today over seven million people in the world enrolled with the sworn purpose of overthrowing society. When it is possible we work through the ballot boxes. In Russia we meet murder with assassination. I speak or think of these assassins as my comrades and would canonize them."[19]

It is significant that London uses the term "revolutionists" almost as often as he does "socialists," and his repeated statement that acts of terrorism may be necessary before the final overthrow of capitalism is certainly close to being an anarchist's solution. London's open flirtation with anarchism was made more disturbing by two events that were still fresh in his readers' minds when London made his Boston speech: the assassination of President William McKinley in 1901 by the anarchist Leon Czolgosz, and the subsequent attempted assassination of Pittsburgh industrialist Henry Clay Frick by Alexander Berkman, the lover of anarchist theorist Emma Goldman. At the end of *The Iron Heel*, London turns Everhard into a terrorist, a development anticipated in the 1901 story "The Minions of Midas" (reprinted in *Moon-Face*), where some intellectual workers blackmail the wealthy by killing people at random. The workers demand tens of millions of dollars, which they intend to use to establish proletarian industries, saying of themselves, "We are the inevitable. We are the culmination of industrial and social wrong. We turn upon the society that has created us."

But London's actual political ideology was not as extreme as it sometimes seems, despite his occasionally paranoid militancy. His definition of socialism as it is reflected in his fiction and essays has been termed muddled and inconsistent, but most of his pronouncements are in essential accord with the definition written into the 1904 Socialist Party platform, which defined socialism as meaning that "all those things upon which the

people in common depend shall by the people in common be held and administered; that all production
shall be for the direct use of the producers."[20] London
favored most of the practical proposals as well: the call
for shorter hours and higher wages, workmen's com-
pensation, pension plans, public ownership of utilities,
a graduated income tax, an expansion of public education programs, and the elimination of child labor.
When Eugene Debs shocked political analysts by gaining half a million votes in the 1904 presidential race,
London said in several articles and interviews that
Debs's achievement was another step in the history of
the class struggle toward a revolutionary new society
based upon order, equity, and justice.

London's commitment to that new order can be
seen in the pleas for social justice that resound through
The Sea-Wolf and *The Iron Heel*. Whatever ideas London
uses, whether it is Kidd's interpretation of Spencer or
Nietzsche's concept of the superman, they are filtered
through his socialist consciousness, as three of his finer
short stories reflect. In "The Dream of Debs" (1909),
the wealthy narrator wakes up in San Francisco with a
feeling that the city is about to be destroyed by another
earthquake. As it turns out, it is a cataclysm of another
kind for him: a general strike by the workers breaks
down the capitalist system in the city. "South of the
Slot" (1909) also takes place in San Francisco. The title
refers to the iron crack, the "Slot," that ran the cable
cars down Market Street and separated the theaters
and banks from the factories and slums. The hero is a
professor of sociology who renounces his academic life
to become a labor leader, fighting for the workers south
of the Slot. And in "The Strength of the Strong" (1911)
London shows primitive men choosing a natural form
of socialism rather than the lies of early capitalism.

The most direct explanation of London's socialist
views is found in the 1903 essay "How I Became a

Socialist," first published in *Comrade* and later included in *War of the Classes*. London begins by saying that socialism was "hammered" into him by his experiences as a tramp, when he saw what the consequences were for workers trapped in the "Social Pit" of the capitalist system where they were "wrenched and distorted and twisted out of shape by toil and hardship and accident, and cast adrift by their masters like old horses." After he returned to California, London says he "opened the books" and read socialist theory, but nothing affected him as profoundly and convincingly, he maintains, "as I was affected on the day when I first saw the walls of the Social Pit rise around me and felt myself slipping down, down, into the shambles at the bottom."

Although London did study Marxian economics and read considerably on related subjects, his socialism never quite became a fixed set of principles. Most likely, he did not actually read much of Marx; it was not until 1906 that Ernest Untermann's first complete English edition was published. But reading Marx extensively would probably not have made much difference. For London, socialism was not so much a system as it was a bitterly held belief stemming from his own fears of returning to the wage slavery of the Social Pit. London's faith in socialism and his hatred for capitalism should be seen as driving forces in his character, rather than as some entirely consistent political philosophy. But as the scholar of Marxism Conrad Zirkle is careful to point out:

London was intellectually honest and logical, and his beliefs were always in accord with his information. He never discarded any idea of importance for the mere reason that it disturbed his tranquility or his philosophy. He was always able to change his philosophical concepts as his knowledge increased and, as long as he lived, he never ceased to grow.[21]

London was proud to point out that he became a

socialist before he was a writer. In many of his speeches
he stressed his working-class origins and liked to depict
himself as an old-time, hard-line party member who
still thought of himself as a member of the proletariat.
One of his greatest apprehensions, as we have seen, is
that the socialist movement would soften its stand on
the need for revolutionary agitation. This is partly
what prompted him to write *The Sea-Wolf*, *The Iron Heel*,
and his other social documents. Much of the effort that
went into these works was directed against the reformist
influences of the middle-class intellectuals who were
taking over the Socialist Party and forgetting about socialism's main objective. Preaching revolution was a
passionate gospel as far as London was concerned, and
however unsystematic he might have been, he tried to
make plain what he wanted. His intention, as he proclaimed in a speech before the student body of the
University of California in 1905, was "to destroy pres-
ent-day civilization, that is, capitalist civilization, with
its brutal struggle of man with man for life . . . and
replace it by a better civilization, a civilization whose
principle shall be 'Each for all and all for Each.'"[22] He
never accomplished this, but there was a time, at least,
when his audience took him at his word.

4

~~~~~~~~~~~~~~~~~~~~~~~~~~~~~~~~~

The Naked Facts of Life

"To know the naked facts of life is not to be pessimistic," London wrote in 1910 to a reporter for the *Honolulu Advertiser*. "Your contention that we must ignore certain unpleasant facts, and dwell on the nice facts, is a sign that you are afraid of a portion of life. And insofar as you run away from a portion of life, by that much will you be ignorant of life."[1]

London was more than willing to face the often sordid details of his life, and he wrote three autobiographical books to prove that he was not afraid to let his readers in on how the "real" Jack London had lived. He did not spare himself in these books. He wrote pretty much the "plain truth," as he remembered it, about his experiences as a tramp, a struggling writer, and an alcoholic. His friends lamented his openness, and George Sterling, for one, could not understand why London, in allowing *The Road* to be published, "gave the mob a mop to bang" him with.[2] After *Martin Eden* came out, preachers across the country attacked London as "a man who failed because of lack of faith in God."[3] And *John Barleycorn* (1913), despite its welcome reception from the Prohibition Party, only served to convince the same preachers of what they already expected: that in addition to being a "godless atheist," London was also a "hopeless drunk." Such reactions distressed London because he had hoped that the books might correct some of the misconceptions that arose as his folk-hero legend expanded. He did not write about

himself to shed his sickness in his books, nor did he
seek to improve his public image. What he wanted to
do, as he said of *John Barleycorn*, was to present the
"bare, bald, absolute fact, a recital of my own personal
experiences."[4]

Autobiography can never quite be such a "recital,"
and no autobiography is ever "the bare, bald, absolute
fact." The recording of a life by one who has lived it has
to be a fictionalization of the personal story to one
degree or another. And autobiography, because it is
essentially a history of changing self-concepts, inevitably turns into the most desperate form of fiction as the
writer tries to seek out the connective threads in the
history of his life. Alfred Kazin speaks from his own
experience on this point: "For the nonfiction writer, as I
can testify, personal history is directly an effort to find
salvation, to make one's own experience come out
right."[5] But the remarkable thing about London as an
autobiographer is that he does not make his experiences "come out right." *The Road* ends with the Frisco
Kid, as London calls himself, highballing it on a freight
to Baltimore, where he has breakfast on his earnings
from a crap game. *Martin Eden* ends with the hero slipping out of a porthole on his Tahiti-bound steamer to
drown himself, laughing aloud as a bonita strikes his
white flesh. And at the end of *John Barleycorn*, London is
still drinking after recounting his adventures, asserting,
"I should not care to revisit all these fair places of the
world except in the fashion I visited them before. *Glass
in hand!*"

Every autobiography implies a theory of human
nature, and Jack London's is a straightforward, unre-
pentant one. For him, environment is the determining
factor in human action. Man is an animal and is at the
mercy of biological determinism. In the essay "What
Life Means to Me" (*Cosmopolitan*, March 1906), London
bluntly states, "My environment was crude and rough

and raw. I had no outlook, but an uplook rather." It is this "uplook" that he spends a lot of time on in his various self-portraits as he depicts his instinctive desire for survival in a hostile world. In the evolutionary scheme of things, certain laws have to be obeyed. Man may be a higher animal, but his survival, like that of all animals, depends on his adaptability — and London always represents himself as a very adaptable animal. But London was not so much a Darwinist as he was a socialist, and in his account of his own life, as in all of his writing, his approach is strongly influenced by his socialist views. This in itself is a justification for his frankness. As he points out in his preface to *War of the Classes*, "Socialism deals with what is, not with what ought to be; and that the material with which it deals is the clay of the common road, the warm human, fallible and frail, sordid and petty, absurd and contradictory, even grotesque, and yet, withal, shot through with flashes and glimmerings of something finer and God-like."

In the second paragraph of *Walden*, Henry David Thoreau writes that he requires "of every writer, first or last, a simple and sincere account of his own life, and not merely what he has heard of other men's lives; some such account as he would send to his kindred from a distant land; for if he has lived sincerely, it must have been in a distant land to me." This is the kind of account London tried to provide, and the life he reveals to us would most certainly have seemed distant to Thoreau and his lonely, penny-pinching existence. But London and Thoreau, however different, are both part of a distinctive tradition in American autobiography, a tradition that basically derives from two patterns. First, there is the Puritan spiritual autobiography, such as Jonathan Edwards's *Personal Narrative* (wr. 1743), that in a confessional manner details the development, as Edwards terms it, of a "sweet inward sense" of one's personal convictions and beliefs. *Walden* is essentially in this category. The second type, represented by Benjamin Franklin's *Autobiography* (wr. 1771–89), provides an account of the subject's worldly progress, and offers tips for attaining the same kind of success. London's autobiographical books do not fit very well into either category. They are somewhat confessional, and he does detail his conversion to socialism, but they center on action rather than contemplation and are hardly "philosophical" after the manner of Edwards or Thoreau. And while London goes into enormous detail in describing how he became a writer, *Martin Eden* is neither a glorification of his accomplishments nor an outline for success. Unlike Franklin, he has no interest in pointing "The Way to Wealth." Instead, he gives a shameless vision of himself that would have been even more forthright if it were not for the restrictions imposed on him by his publishers regarding "improper" material.

George Brett of Macmillan objected to the publication of *The Road* for just such a reason, maintaining that the book would seem disreputable and might actually hurt London in the marketplace. In his reply London said that even if Brett could provide him with good evidence that bringing out *The Road* would hurt the sale of the other books, it would not change his mind. London argued that the "consistent and true picture" of himself that he had tried to build up in *The Road* and in all of his work was his biggest asset and should help make the book a commercial success.[6] Brett turned out to be right. *The Road* was attacked for its depiction of shifty-eyed tramps, even though London is today regarded as the first writer to portray the tramp phenomenon in America with any degree of accuracy. One reviewer even objected to the quality of the writing: "He is too smooth a story-teller to be altogether plausible and he takes such manifest delight in his skill and success as a liar when he was beating his way across the continent that we involuntarily wonder at what date he abandoned the habit."[7] Given the many unfair reviews, the book did not sell well, and Macmillan wound up remaindering it.

London could understand why the book might prove to be distasteful to many readers, but he could not accept the objections of those who thought the book would damage his character. Because of his belief that *The Road* was a truthful depiction of what he had done, London complained that he could not "get a line on" why some of his friends wished he had not written it.[8] What London probably did not realize was that however honest he had intended to be, the book was perceived as little more than a scandalously bad example for American youth. But London was not at all concerned with examples. In most autobiographies, the writer's relation to the reader becomes didactic because experiences are being held up as examples of what or what not to do. *The Road*, however, is simply what its title promises: what happened to London when he went "over the cold crests of the Sierras" in 1894 on his eight-month tramping journey through the United States and Canada.

While full of fascinating detail of what such an adventure was like during the depression years of the 1890s, *The Road* is not a diary-like chronicle of London's tramping days. The book is divided into nine sections, each detailing a part of London's adventure, but not in chronological order. "Confession" tells how he learned to survive by "throwing his feet" for meals and panhandling for money. The next three chapters explain the finer points of riding the rails, detail the more pleasantly memorable pictures of "Hobo Land," and describe how London got "pinched" for vagrancy by a "fly cop" in Niagara Falls, New York. At the center of the book is Chapter Five, "The Pen," which gives

London's horrifying account of his month in the Erie
County Penitentiary. The remaining four chapters represent a narrative ascent of sorts, as London writes
about pursuing the mysterious "Skysail Jack" in a race
across Canada on the rails, justifies why he went on the
road in the first place ("because of the life that was in
me"), recounts his earlier adventures with Kelly's Army, and comments on how he adapted to life outside
the law by outwitting the railroad cops.

The book provides an image of London as a resourceful adventurer who is able to witness and endure
the most degrading scenes — and live to tell about them.
He writes of getting along with "petty crooks and
tinhorns, to say nothing of a vast and hungry horde of
hoboes." He tells of lying to the police in Winnipeg to
avoid another vagrancy charge. He confesses that he
helplessly watched a gypsy woman get beaten nearly to
death outside Harrisburg, Pennsylvania. "Well, and
what of it?" he asks. "It was a page out of life, that's all;
and there are many pages far worse, that I have seen."
Pages out of the penitentiary, for example, where he
survived by putting himself under the protection of an
older prisoner, "a brute-beast, wholly unmoral," and
where he learned to deal with a huge, illiterate five-year
veteran of Sing Sing who trapped sparrows and ate
them raw, "crunching bones and spitting out feathers."
In the following chapters, London proves a central
point again and again: that "it is no snap to strike a
strange town, broke, at midnight, in cold weather, and
find a place to sleep." London explains how he became
road-smart, but he never makes himself out to be a
hero. As a consequence, the book is a masterpiece of
low-keyed self-analysis that never belabors its reason
for being. "I went on 'The Road' because I couldn't
keep away from it," London says; "because I hadn't the
price of the railroad fare in my jeans, because I was so
made that I couldn't work all my life on 'one same shift';
because — well just because it was easier to than not to."

*   *   *

Martin Eden, even though it is a novel rather than straight autobiography, is more deliberately introspective. It is, in a sense, like the series of prefaces Henry James wrote for the New York edition of his works. The prefaces, James said, "represent, over a considerable course, the continuity of an artist's endeavor, the growth of his whole operative consciousness." In one sense, *Martin Eden* develops as a *Bildungsroman*, or education novel; but in another and more important sense, it is an attempt at portraying the development of the artistic consciousness in an economic system that insists on valuing the artist as just another commodity in the marketplace. London had contemplated a novel on such a topic for more than a decade before he finally began work on *Martin Eden* in 1907. What resulted is by no means a point-for-point summary of London's youthful struggles; London compresses twelve years of his own life into three for Martin, and he transforms the Klondike gold rush into a treasure-hunting venture in the South Seas. But the compression greatly intensifies the monomania of the hero. "My desire to write is the greatest thing in me," Martin proclaims.

At the start of his story, Martin lives in a world where the very air is "repulsive and mean," but he is "keenly sensitive" to beauty and has an imagination through which he constantly sees "arrayed around his consciousness endless pictures from his life." That life has been raw and mean, and he has survived a hundred fights and beatings only to realize that as soon as his money is gone he will have to go to sea again. His luck changes, however, when he rescues Arthur Morse from a street brawl and is invited to Morse's splendid home as a reward. Twenty-one years old, and wearing "rough clothes that smacked of the sea," Martin is dazzled by the refinement he encounters in the Morse home. He is so self-conscious that he is afraid to walk around in the house for fear of breaking some expensive ornament. He is even more awkward when he meets Arthur's delicately beautiful sister, Ruth. "Here was intellectual life," London writes of Martin, "and here was beauty, warm and wonderful as he had never dreamed it could be. He forgot himself and stared at her with hungry eyes. Here was something to live for, to win to, to fight for — ay, and die for."

Ruth lends "wings to his imagination." She becomes a female Pygmalion to him and tries to shape him into "the image of her ideal man." He studies books of etiquette, learns English grammar as if he is encountering a foreign language, gives up his habit of handrolling cigarettes out of Mexican tobacco, and even rehearses the way he walks so that he can eliminate the unmistakable rolling gait of the sailor. Like London himself, Martin is a voracious reader and, with Ruth's encouragement and her university-educated example, he soon becomes an expert on the fashionable literature of the day as well as the deeper stuff of Marx and Spencer. But as his education progresses, he begins to understand that Ruth is simply trying to impress upon him the bourgeois virtues she sees in her father's friend Mr. Butler. Starting out on a salary of three dollars a week in a printing office, Butler has become a "great man" with an income of thirty thousand a year by practicing "renunciation, sacrifice, patience, industry, and high endeavor." But the more he reads, the more Martin begins to see through the hypocrisy in Ruth's world and the spiritual paltriness in Butler's career.

As Martin becomes increasingly proficient in his studies, he begins to debate and defeat the professors who visit the Morse household. In these scenes Martin comes close to the boorishness of Ernest Everhard in *The Iron Heel*, and Ruth at times approaches Maud Brewster of *The Sea-Wolf* in her excessive gentility. The Morse family tries to discourage Ruth's interest in Martin, particularly when he rents a typewriter, moves to a small back room in the house of a Portuguese washerwoman, and begins a frenzied life of pounding out manuscripts on five hours' sleep a night while slowly starving. He studies the magazines, analyzes the literary markets, and writes anything he thinks will bring in a few dollars. The manuscripts go out and come back. He pawns his bicycle and his overcoat. He takes a job in a laundry, but cannot stand the fourteen-hour days. He misses rent payments on his typewriter. All the while, Ruth keeps at him to get a steady job, to go into business and work his way up as Mr. Butler did.

Through all of this, his only friend, the cynical poet and socialist Russ Brissenden (patterned on George Sterling), is his sole encouragement. When Martin, through a newspaperman's willful mistake, develops an unearned reputation as a revolutionary, Ruth drops him. Brissenden, his own literary career in trouble, commits suicide just before his greatest poem becomes a national success. And then, when all of Martin's efforts seem pointless, the magazines start to buy his stories and essays. Almost overnight, he becomes a commodity, something of value, something to sell, and Ruth comes back, trying to tell him she has loved him all along. He rejects her and tries briefly to return to the working-class world of his earlier love, Lizzie Connolly, but it is no use. He lapses into a strange passive disenchantment, decides to escape the disillusionment success has brought him, and boards the fatal steamer for Tahiti.

Martin Eden's story is a dark one, and he pays a heavy price for his success. His last name indicates London's recurrent use of the *Paradise Lost* motifs that run through most of his work. Martin possesses the Garden of Eden within his consciousness as an artist and, as his development is chronicled, Ruth becomes his Eve, offering him the knowledge that bourgeois society at that time ordinarily withheld from the working-class Adam. As his consciousness expands, it turns into

what Lizzie Connolly calls a "think machine." Like
Wolf Larsen in the throes of a headache, Martin wishes
that he had never opened the books, had never responded to the "tinkling silver bells" of Ruth's voice and
laughter. Martin's failure is essentially the same as Larsen's, and London himself provided the appropriate
interpretation. "Being an individualist, being unaware
of the needs of others, of the whole collective human
need, Martin Eden lived only for himself, fought only
for himself, and, if you please, died for himself," London wrote in an open letter defending the novel. "He
fought for entrance into the bourgeois circles where he
expected to find refinement, culture, high-living and
high thinking. He won his way into those circles and
was appalled by the colossal, unlovely mediocrity of the
bourgeoisie."[10] When Martin learned that love had
tricked and failed him, and that all of the things he had
attained meant nothing to him, "being a consistent Individualist, being unaware of the collective human
need, there remained nothing for which to live and
fight. And so he died."

London was, of course, confronting himself in
Martin. The novel was written during the cruise of the
Snark, when London was in the midst of seemingly impossible financial difficulties. It was as if the farther he
sailed from California, the more unreal his accomplishments became and the more his problems compounded
themselves. As he traced his own history in the life of
Martin, London became more critical of the American
dream of success. London had become a divided self as
his ambitions soared and his money problems mounted, and much of the hackwork he was forced to do just
to get the *Snark* afloat increased the very anxiety he had
gone to the South Seas to escape. He began to question
his own achievement, and like Martin started to wonder if he had not indeed become false, simply a newspaper personality. "He drove along the path of relentless

logic to the conclusion that he was nobody, nothing," London writes; "Martin Eden, the famous writer, was a vapor that had arisen from the mob mind."

The novel is a document in despair, and in reading it we are hit hard by the distress in the narrative voice. Yet sincerity is behind it all, however harsh and unfair London may have been in his depiction of Sterling as Brissenden and Mabel Applegarth as Ruth. Here is a novel in which the writer admits that something has gone terribly wrong with his life. This is as much an account of the death of artistic consciousness as it is one of growth.

Unlike his alter ego, London did survive his neurasthenic crisis. A few years later he explained how and why in a letter to Mary Banks Krasky, an author who had written to praise *The Star Rover*. London told her that he indeed did go through Martin Eden's experience, but that socialism and his social conscience helped him to avoid Martin's suicide.[11] Many critics have questioned London's commitment to socialism, and others have argued that Brissendon's attempts at making Martin into a socialist are too incoherent to have any effect. But there can be little doubt that London himself believed that his social consciousness had saved him, even though the glimpses into his personality that he affords in *Martin Eden* are distressingly unflattering.

Brett had warned against publishing the book, just as he had concerning the release of *The Road*. And again he was right; the notices were not good, largely because the reviewers could not appreciate what London, "the famous writer," had gone through to get where he was. Martin's progress as Ruth improves his manners is amazing, but London actually experienced the same awakening in his contacts with the Applegarth family. Nonetheless, *Current Literature* scoffed at the way "the blunt sailor, by a marvelous transformation, is changed

into a bookworm."[12] The point the reviewer missed is
that for London such a change did, in fact, occur. His
actual development after he returned to Oakland after
his eight months on the road was so rapid that it is
understandable why critics would be incredulous after
reading London's account of it in *Martin Eden*—they
failed to comprehend what London had been up
against. They also missed the writer's purpose. *Martin
Eden* is as much an attack on the capitalist system and
the publishing industry as it is a veiled autobiography.
London's own appraisal of the novel in this respect
turned out to be true: "It will not make me any
friends." [13]

The long-suffering George Brett did not have to worry
about London's alienating critics and readers with *John
Barleycorn*, the writer's strongest autobiographical statement and his most painfully honest. London became
unhappy with Macmillan around 1912 because the
company had mishandled the photographs for *The
Cruise of the Snark*; he also thought his publisher was no
longer promoting his books adequately. As a consequence, London worked out a contract with Century
Company, which published *John Barleycorn* and three of
his other books before he went back to Macmillan with
The Valley of the Moon. But no matter what publisher
would handle *John Barleycorn*, London was determined
to write it, partly in response to the critics who had
accused him of striking a false note with his personal
representation in *Martin Eden*. "In three years, from a
sailor with a common school education, I made a successful writer of him," London says of Martin midway
through *John Barleycorn*.

Yet I was Martin Eden. At the end of three working years,
two of which were spent in high school and the university and
one spent at writing, and all three in studying immensely and

intensely, I was publishing stories in magazines such as the *Atlantic Monthly*, was correcting proofs of my first book . . . was selling sociological articles to *Cosmopolitan* and *McClure's*, had declined an associate editorship proferred me from New York City, and was getting ready to marry.

Although all of this may sound like bragging, in the context of the calmly analytical text of London's alcoholic memoirs it works as plainly stated fact.

In describing *John Barleycorn* to his new editor at Century Company in 1912 (the title of the book derives from a slang term for strong drink at the time), London wrote: "It is the personal autobiographical discussion of the drink question from A to Z."[14]

London drank heavily throughout most of his life, but the immediate motivation for the book came out of a binge he went on during the winter of 1911, when he took Charmian with him on a business trip to New York. Leaving her alone most mornings in an apartment on Morningside Heights, he spent his days and nights with a roistering pack of friends who hauled him off to the saloons of Broadway. He went to boxing matches, was seen in the company of chorus girls, and announced to a reporter that a city such as ancient Rome at its wildest could not compare with New York.[15] For one of the few times in his professional life, he stopped writing. The maelstrom of drinking finally had its effect on his stomach, and he promised Charmian that he would quit drinking when they boarded the clipper *Dirigo* for their return trip to California via Cape Horn. While on the voyage he vowed he would fulfill another promise: to write a book about his drinking in an effort to come to grips with his problem. But first he would go on one more drunk before the March sailing date. Sometime during his debauch, he had his head shaved completely bald; he also had himself photographed standing by the grave of Edgar Allan Poe.

But the voyage was five months long, there was no liquor aboard, and he got back to his writing. "I have learned to my absolute satisfaction," he said to Charmian, "that *I am not an alcoholic* in any sense of the word."[16]

Toward the end of his career, London began announcing to his editors that each new book was either the greatest of its kind or some new departure of one sort or another. All of these claims, with one exception, were smoke screens for bad work. But what he said to William Ellsworth of Century Company about *John Barleycorn* was no exaggeration. "I may venture to point out," London wrote, "that *John Barleycorn* is unlike any other book ever published anywhere in this world."[17]

London's incredibly detailed history of his battle with the bottle begins as one thing and ends up as another. He justifies the work at the start as a temperance tract, he traces his steady slide toward the depths of alcoholic depression when he is overwhelmed by what he terms the "White Logic," and he ends with a nostalgic tribute to the many watering holes he has visited in Venice, London, Santiago, New Orleans, and San Francisco — all "visions of bright congregating-places of men, and the jollity of raised glasses, and of song and cheer and the hum of genial voices." The reviewer in *The Nation* was quick to notice the amusing contradiction in the memoir: "As a tract against the saloon, and a professed argument for woman suffrage in order that the saloon may be done away with, it will please the prohibitionists and suffragists. As a record of glorious sprees and multifarious good-fellowship, it is capable of exciting thirst in the thirst-minded."[18]

London's reminiscences in *John Barleycorn* begin with an election day when he had ridden from his ranch into town to vote on some amendments to the Constitution of the State of California. "Because of the warmth of the day I had several drinks before casting my ballot," he writes, "and divers drinks after casting it. Then

I had ridden up through the vine-clad hills and rolling pastures of the ranch and arrived at the farmhouse in time for another drink and supper." Charmian wanted to know about how he had voted on the amendment for equal suffrage. When London announced that he had gone for it, she almost fell over — and not because London opposed feminism. The woman suffrage issue was tied in with the prohibition issue, the assumption being that when women got the ballot they would vote for prohibition. Given London's long friendship with John Barleycorn, Charmian could only conclude that her husband must have been drunk when he cast his ballot.

"I continued to talk," London explains. "As I say, I was lighted up. In my brain every thought was at home. Every thought, in its little cell, crouched ready-dressed at the door, like prisoners at midnight waiting a jail-break. And every thought was a vision, bright-imaged, sharp-cut, unmistakable. My brain was il-luminated by the clear, white light of alcohol." He out-lined his life to Charmian, told her that he was "no hereditary alcoholic," that he had always drunk whiskey only for its "kick," not for its taste, and that he had learned to drink only through years of "unwilling ap-prenticeship." Had alcohol not been accessible, he would never have gotten started drinking, and would never have missed it. Only a few people are born in each generation with body chemistries that crave alco-hol, London argued; the rest of the drinkers simply learn the habit the way they learn to smoke.

"The women know the game," he said to Char-mian.

They pay for it — the wives and sisters and mothers. And when they come to vote they will vote for prohibition. And the best of it is that there will be no hardship worked on the coming generation. Not having access to alcohol, not being predisposed toward alcohol, it will never miss alcohol. It will

mean life more abundant for the manhood of the young boys
born and growing up—ay, and life more abundant for the
young girls born and growing up to share the lives of the
young men.

Charmian's suggestion at the conclusion of London's
sermon was that London should someday write about
his "long years of rubbing shoulders" with John Barleycorn. But when London did sit down to write, he did
not produce the kind of guidebook for the young that
Charmian expected. Instead, London wrote an intimate biography of his own addictive personality, bla-
tantly setting forth the obsessional nature that made
him both a compulsive writer and a compulsive drinker.
London opens his narrative by sketching his "first
intoxications and revulsions," telling how he got drunk
on beer when he was five years old, and how he lapsed
into delirium at seven after drinking wine at an Italian
rancho "on the bleak sad coast of San Mateo County
south of San Francisco." Even though he had a "physical loathing for alcohol," the brightest spots in his dismal childhood were the saloons, whose doors were always open to him; and it was in the saloons that he
grew up. Much of the book is devoted to loving descriptions of the bars London patronized. Everywhere he
went he found saloons, "on highway and byway, up
narrow alleys and on busy thoroughfares, bright-light-
ed and cheerful, warm in winter and in summer dark
and cool. Yes, the saloon was a mighty fine place, and it
was more than that." By the time he was sixteen and
roaming San Francisco Bay as an oyster pirate, he was
spending most of his money on steam beer and shots at
the First and Last Chance, earning a reputation as a
good fellow ashore with his money—"buying drinks like
a man." Drinking was a way of life for the men with
whom he lived, men who "dated existence from drunk
to drunk." Not even his near-drowning in the Car-

quinez Straits sobered him up. Wherever he ranged, "the way lay along alcohol-drenched roads." Months at sea on the *Sophie Sutherland* straightened him out, but as soon as the ship put in at the Bonin Islands and later at Yokohama, he went "mad with drink." His drinking continued when he returned to Oakland and went on the road: "Even a tramp, in those halcyon days, could get most frequently drunk."

London downplays his Klondike drinking, claiming that the quart of whiskey in his "personal medicine chest" was opened only once: when a doctor in a lonely camp had to operate without anesthetics (the doctor got half of the bottle, the patient the other half). As London's writing career began to take off during his first marriage, he started to drink Scotch highballs with his friends, and he and George Sterling would spend afternoons in London's den matching each other drink for drink. This was his "most dangerous stage when a man believes himself John Barleycorn's master," London writes. After his "long sickness," his desire for alcohol became more "a mental need, a nerve need, a good-spirits need." When he would go aboard the *Spray* for a day's cruise, he would take a couple of gallons of whiskey. When he moved to the ranch after his marriage to Charmian, he got an Oakland barkeeper to make cocktails in bulk and ship them to him. He tried to go without drinking on the *Snark* but, when he reached the Marquesas, he was "the possessor of a real, man's size thirst," and at Tahiti he "outfitted with Scotch and American whiskey." Back in California, he began looking for a guest to have a cocktail with him each morning after working. One day, no guest present, he took a cocktail anyway. "And right there John Barleycorn had me," London testifies. "I was beginning to drink regularly. I was beginning to drink alone."

He had trouble sleeping, and began taking a "bracer" before breakfast so he could work. His body was never free from alcohol, and sooner or later, as London puts it, "the freight has to be paid." It is then that "John Barleycorn sends his White Logic, the argent messenger of truth beyond truth, the antithesis of life, cruel and bleak as interstellar space, pulseless and frozen as absolute zero, dazzling with the frost of irrefragable logic and unforgettable fact." When the brain is soaked with alcohol, the White Logic brings on "the cosmic sadness that has always been the heritage of man," and London was shocked into an awareness of his own disintegrating flesh. The White Logic made it impossible for him to appreciate the beautiful setting of his ranch; in the beauty of nature he saw only "the piteous tragic play of life feeding on life." Everything turned into a cosmic joke, and the book-walled den he had loved became "the mausoleum of the thoughts of men."

London is unsparing in his treatment of his descent into the embrace of the White Logic, candidly saying: "To the best of my power I have striven to give the reader a glimpse of a man's secret dwelling when it is shared by John Barleycorn." The result is a starkly confessional reliquary of forlorn resolutions and broken promises. But London also reveals how his writing and his drinking derived from the same impulses. From the start, London's vision of human nature was a grim one, and all of his best fiction moves downward to a moment of confrontation with the White Logic, no matter what situational premise London is treating. Darwinism was enough to elicit that moment in his stories; alcohol brought it about in his life. And when the two merged, as they apparently did in the writing of London's darkest books — such as *Martin Eden* — the cosmic sadness distills from London's imagination at one-hundred proof.

The concluding chapter of *John Barleycorn* presents London's final thoughts on his life as a drinking man,

and it is not quite what the prohibitionists wanted. Although he favors prohibition, he says he will still take his drink — on occasion. "With all the books on my shelves, with all the thoughts of the thinkers shaded by my particular temperament," he reasons, "I decided coolly and deliberately that I should continue to do what I had been trained to want to do. I would drink — but, oh, more skillfully, more discreetly, than ever before. Never again would I be a peripatetic conflagration. Never again would I invoke the White Logic. I had learned how not to invoke him." As London's remaining years proved, this is pure rationalization, but there is a wonderfully delicious appeal in London's image of himself as he muses over the "purple passages and freedoms" John Barleycorn has afforded him: "I persuade I see myself again drinking cocktails on the cool *lannais*, and fizzes out at Waikiki where the surf rolls in."

As it turned out, the book that George Brett feared would damage London the most was one of the best-sellers of 1913. The Prohibition Party, the Young Christian Temperance Union, and the Women's Temperance Union went as mad over it as London had over his beer in Yokohama. Part of the London legend is that when he got the first report on orders and sales, he toasted the book's success by taking a long pull from a bottle of Scotch.

London refused all offers to lecture, and there is some evidence that he had a little fun with the prohibitionists. He agreed to serve as vice-president of the National Defense Association, a weird collection of individuals, bound together in the best American tradition of naive extremism, that had drafted a "No Drunkard Bill" they were trying to persuade the New York State Legislature to pass. The idea was to license drinkers, allowing each person two drunks a year. A third spree would mean loss of license. London told a reporter, "I am absolutely convinced that the no drunkard plan is the finest thing that has yet been presented, considered in the light of the circumstances, for the abolition of drinking."[19] Undoubtedly, this was said with a wink.

The main impact of *John Barleycorn* remains the same as that of London's other autobiographical books: the recital of the "bare, bald, absolute fact" turns into surprisingly merciless self-criticism. No writer of autobiography can dare to tell all about himself, and late in 1913 London acknowledged as much concerning *John Barleycorn*: "All that is in it is true; but I did not dare put in the whole truth."[20] Maybe not, but he comes close. At a time when publishers discouraged candid depictions of fictional characters, London insisted on telling his life story "straight from the shoulder," giving us his primitive and unmediated self. "I am still firm in my belief that my strength lies in being candid, in being true to myself as I am today, and also being true to myself as I was at six, sixteen, and twenty-six," London wrote to George Brett in defense of *The Road*. "Who am I to be ashamed of what I have experienced? I have become what I am because of my past."[21]

5

Working-Class Writer

To Jack London, as he said in giving advice to a young writer in 1914, the one special advantage of authorship as a livelihood is that he could keep his office and business under his hat and go anywhere and write anywhere—so long as the debts were paid.[1] Always eager to answer letters from literary aspirants, London seldom gave them the standard caution to "write about what you know." Instead, he encouraged them to read more and enlarge their own imaginative possibilities. This was a principle London held himself to throughout his life, and he never was willing to limit himself to a single genre or restrict his choice of subject matter. On the contrary, his range is so great that even a quick look at the London bibliography—stories, essays, novels, autobiography, travel sketches, and several remarkably forgettable plays—is enough to convince the reader that here indeed is "some dexterous and strident Barnum of the printed word."[2] To London, authorship meant the freedom to go where he wanted and to write about whatever came to mind or turned up—so long as it would pay. The truly astounding amount of writing London put out in his forty years has led to the unfortunate conclusion that his lesser-known writing—his South Sea stories, his fantasy novels, and his sports fiction and sports writing—is essentially hackwork. But even when writing at top speed, with deadlines to be met and staggering debts to be paid, London was a

surprisingly careful writer who sought to "pour out in
the printed speech the joy of his heart."[3]

Jack London's adventurous life has been popularly
associated with the Klondike for so many decades
that his other travels, both physical and transcendental,
are all too often overlooked in estimates of his importance. It is thus somewhat startling to realize that a
much greater part of London's life was spent traveling
through the South Seas than was spent mushing
through the Klondike, and that eleven of his books are
at least partly set in Hawaii, Tahiti, the Solomon Islands, and other parts of the Pacific.[4] From the time he
sailed on the *Sophie Sutherland* in 1893 until his final trip
to Honolulu in 1916, London found the Pacific to be an
especially purposeful setting for his fiction. The work
that came out of his various voyages westward from San
Francisco resembles his Klondike stories in some ways,
and his characters again have to deal with an environment that is unpredictable and unforgiving, although
typhoons and unbearable sunlight take the place of
blizzards and the White Silence. But the Pacific stories,
as violent and dark in mood as they often are, usually
have a softened tone as the narrator laments the tendency of white developers to turn such places as
Melville's Valley of the Typee into junkyards, and to
turn the once fiercely independent natives into slave
laborers for the copra plantations.

London tended to discount his South Sea stories,
and before the *Snark* cast off he said that he was leaving
California for pure fun of adventure, not for the sake
of literature. "I'd rather win a water-fight in the
swimming pool, or remain astride a horse that is trying
to get out from under me, than write the great American novel," he proclaimed. "Each man to his
liking. . . . That is why I am building the *Snark*. I am
so made. I like, that is all. The trip around the world
means big moments of living."[5]

No great novel came directly out of the voyage, except for *Martin Eden*, which uses the South Seas only incidentally at the end. *Adventure* (1911) is a story of a Solomon Islands planter and his involvement with an exaggerated heroine (it relies on *A Daughter of the Snows* for too much of its characterization). *The Mutiny of the Elsinore* (1914) is a rewrite of *The Sea-Wolf*, involving a captain and first mate who make up a composite Wolf Larsen, and a cabin boy and a captain's daughter who resemble Humphrey Van Weyden and Maud Brewster, respectively; the two lovers actually sail off into the sunset together. And the posthumous dog novels, *Jerry of the Islands* and *Michael, Brother of Jerry* (both 1917), can be read only as the potboilers they were when London concocted them. The thirty or so short stories are another matter, however, and some of them do reflect the "big moments of living" present in London's best writing.

At its most pleasing, London's Pacific is a "riot of color and pounding surf," its islands and atolls places where one can live life "as the best of us may live it."[b] But as much as London looked upon the South Seas as a magic world of brilliant color and magical escape to the exotic haunts of Melville, Stevenson, and Gauguin, his expectations were dashed near the start of his *Snark* adventure when he visited the leper colony at Molokai. Such places seemed to him to be immediate reminders of a theme that had appeared in his fiction for years: the exploitation of native peoples by outsiders, who not only bring corruption and disease, but refuse to take any responsibility for the consequences.

"Koolau the Leper" (*The House of Pride*, 1912) is a story London wrote in response to what he witnessed on Molokai. In a manner reminiscent of "The League of the Old Men," a band of lepers resists being forced off their native island and imprisoned on Molokai. After inevitably futile resistance, only Koolau, having eluded the pursuing soldiers and authorities for two years, is left: "Across his chest he laid his Mauser rifle, lingering affectionately for a moment to wipe the dampness from the barrel. The hand with which he wiped had no fingers left upon it with which to pull the trigger." Once again, the overplayed and largely false charge that London was an out-and-out racist is negated by his avowed sympathy for exploited peoples, no matter whether they are Polynesians or Siwash Indians.

London's attitude toward the Pacific setting in his stories was, of course, greatly affected by the loathsome troubles he and his crew endured after leaving Hawaii. His collection of tropical diseases had gotten so bad by the time he reached the Solomon Islands that the very air seemed saturated with poison. The Melanesians impressed him as cannibals who calculated their profit and loss in homicides. And most of the white men he met had been made sick by the whiskey, the sun, and the moral turpitude that long exposure to the tropics induced. London's white characters in his most oppressive South Sea stories are unable to develop the kind of code of survival that is so important in the Malemute Kid stories. And some of these white men, such as Max Bunster in "Mauki" (*South Sea Tales*, 1911) are reduced to ironic representations of Western values run aground, leading to the conclusion London offers in *The Cruise of the Snark* (1911) that, in such instances, "the white race flourishes on impurity and corruption."

Bunster is a German, "a bully and a coward, and a thrice-bigger savage than any savage on the island" of Lord Howe, where he is the representative of the Moongleam Soap Company and the only Caucasian. Somewhat like Black Leclère of "Bâtard," Bunster is locked into a hellish "marriage" of brutality with his servant, Mauki, the son of a chief. Bunster entertains himself by beating Mauki's head against a wall, stabbing him with a burning cigar, and scarifying his flesh with a mitten made from the sandpaper-like skin of a stingray. Like the "devil dog" of London's earlier story, Mauki waits patiently for his vengeance. When Bunster is brought down by blackwater fever, Mauki takes the mitten and flays Bunster alive. As Mauki is readying a boat for his escape, "a hideous, skinless thing came out of the house and ran screaming down the beach till it fell in the sand and mowed and gibbered under the scorching sun. Mauki looked toward it and hesitated. Then he went over and removed the head, which he wrapped in a net and stowed in the stern-locker of the cutter."

Not all of London's white men in the South Sea stories are like Bunster, however, and in *A Son of the Sun* (1912) London tries to coordinate his tales by linking them to David Grief, a blue-eyed adventurer who somewhat resembles Smoke Bellew transported to the tropics. Grief, like Bellew and the Malemute Kid, is a moral force serving to remind other men of their lost sense of pride and decency, and he occasionally steps in to provide direct solutions to problems. But his presence makes the story-by-story progression seem needlessly artificial, and in some of the stories, such as "The Terrible Solomons," he hardly seems to have any narrative purpose at all.

After the immediate effects of London's tropical ailments had passed, and particularly from 1914 when he again began to look at the South Seas — most particularly, Hawaii — as a place of refuge if not real adventure, his attitude toward his Pacific material changed. This can be somewhat attributed to his reading of Freud and Jung. But Richard O'Connor's suggestion that London tried "at the last moment to make the transition from Marxist to Freudian and thereby save himself, like a man sliding down the face of a cliff and grabbing at rocks and bushes to save his fall"[7] is too

dramatic an explanation. London's final South Sea stories, published in *The Red One* (1918) and *On the Makaloa
Mat* (1919) are definitely more intentionally literary
than most of the preceding ones. The last story he
wrote, "The Water Baby," for example, has a static psychological structure to it as an old fisherman articulates
Polynesian religious beliefs that take us beyond the language of dreams to "knowledge of the language of fishes." London does allude specifically to the ideas of
Freud in "The Kanuka Surf," and other stories do seem
to draw on Jung's explanations of nonrational thought.
But as much as anything, his South Seas stories in their
final phase show him turning back to a more mellow
version of his patented method of taking local gossip
and barroom stories and working them out in reference
to his reading.

This is certainly what happens with "When Alice
Told Her Soul," a mildly comic story about a woman
who has run a "hula house" and is talked into repenting
by an evangelist. She wants "rebirth," but first she must
make a public confession. And when she does, she inadvertently tells more about the sins of her exclusive
Honolulu patrons than she does about her own indis-
cretions. Another story, "The Bones of Kahekili," centers on an anecdote of the islands and reintroduces a
standard London character: an aging white plantation
owner whose illusions have been dissipated long since
by drink. He asks Kamuhana, an old servant, to tell
him about the burial of the legendary Chief Kahekili.
Kamuhana narrates a story about how as a young man
he was selected to accompany the body of the chief out
to sea as a human sacrifice. But when the coffin was
thrown overboard, it failed to sink. As was the custom,
it had a glass cover, which a horrified priest was forced
to break. Kamuhana escaped in the confusion, and he
alone is able to tell the story. This is one of London's
best tales of terror, and he apparently tells it mainly as

a way of underscoring the often tragic beauty of the
South Seas as he had come to understand it at the end.
And it is full of the flashingly poetic imagery that the
Pacific evoked from him. As London wrote in a 1915
letter he sent to Joseph Conrad in praise of the latter's
novel *Victory*, which London had stayed up all night
reading: "The mynah birds are waking the hot dawn
about me. The surf is thundering in my ears where it
falls on the white sand of the beach, here at
Waikiki. . . . This night has been yours — and mine."[8]

For a writer who often complained that he lacked origi-
nality and had a difficult time coming up with ideas for
stories, London wrote a great deal of what is now called
fantasy fiction. And some of his South Seas stories,
with their excursions into Polynesian folklore and fan-
cy, almost fit into this category. Although London believed that all of his work should be grounded in reality
and "researched," his imagination, particularly in three
novels — *Before Adam* (1906), *The Scarlet Plague* (1915),
and *The Star Rover* (1915) — sometimes carried him a
long way from his starting point.

In these books, London demonstrates his reliance
on a kind of "automatic" writing that suggests a lingering interest in the spiritualism forced on him by his
mother, and also reveals a dimension of personality
that London went to considerable pains to deny. In
remarking on *The Star Rover*, for instance, London said
that for all of the novel's emphasis on the transmigra-
tion of souls and out-of-body experiences, the book is
partly a literary hoax. As London explained to Roland
Phillips of *Cosmopolitan*, the novel is full of pseudo-scientific tricks that London has played with such ideas as
the power of mind over matter — ideas that were then
being popularized by the Christian Science and New
Thought movements.[9] But however much London protested, the novel demonstrates an unmuted interest in

ghost stories, the spiritual world, the origins of primitive fears, and the power of dreams — all of which shows
up in his three fantasy novels and has glimmerings in
much of his earlier fiction.

   Before Adam begins with the narrator's complaint
about being tormented by "a procession of nightmares"
in his childhood, and goes on to tell of a recurrent
dream he has of himself as the pre-human Big-Tooth,
who lives in the mid-Pleistocene Age. His tribe, known
as the Folk, are the "missing link" between the Tree
People and homo sapiens, the Fire People. Like the
heroes of many London stories, Big-Tooth and his
friend Lop-Ear run away on a journey toward maturity
that takes them to the "high backbone of earth" and
down into a valley of riches, the streams "packed thick
with salmon" and the grasslands incredibly fertile. The
pilgrimage is circular, in a sense, and Big-Tooth eventually rejoins the Folk and takes the Swift One as his
mate. When attacked by the Fire People, Big-Tooth
and the Swift One must flee into a swamp, but they live
to raise a family. London does not trace the descent of
man, but the narrator says: "One thing only is certain,
and that is that Big-Tooth did stamp into the cerebral
constitution of one of his progeny all the impressions of
his life, and stamped them in so indelibly that the hosts
of intervening generations have failed to obliterate
them."

   The novel ends with what seems to be a statement
of literal belief in primal memory, but London covered
for himself by pointing out that most of the time he
slept "like a babe" and that the book offered proof of
several theories he had regarding human prehistory.
London argued, in a letter to a fellow socialist who had
asked about the book's purpose, that *Before Adam* had
been written to show the slow development of primitive
man. London pointed out that the novel demonstrates
how the process of biological evolution resulted in "mis-

takes and lost off-shoots," and that in a single generation the most likely device his prehistoric characters
could have invented was the use of gourds to carry
water and berries.[10] This may be so, and London certainly did write to correct some of the errors of other
writers in the "caveman" stories that were popular at the
time, but it is the romance of the "unknown ages" that
carries the story and makes it one of the most read-
able of London's minor works. "As a half-grown boy, I
reveled in the book, opening as it did vast vistas of the
human past with which I was unfamiliar," Loren Eiseley testifies. "Reading it today as a professional anthro-
pologist, I find that none of that old thrill has
departed. . . . The great swamp that is the scene of
Big-Tooth's final flight, that waste which caused my
flesh to creep even as a boy, I as a man now mentally
perceive as a symbol of man's long journey, harried by
his own ferocity from age to age."[11]

At the end of *Before Adam*, Big-Tooth's mortal enemy, Red-Eye, who seems like some throwback even
within the Folk, takes a mate among the Tree People.
This obsession with atavism shows up in many of London's works, but no more disturbingly than in *The Scarlet Plague*. The novel's hero, James Howard Smith, a
former professor of English at Berkeley, lives through
an epidemic in 2013 A.D. and then begins wandering
through California looking for other survivors. Near
Lake Temascal he meets "the Chauffeur," who is large
and hairy, heavy-jawed and slant-browed, a physical
replica of Red-Eye from *Before Adam*. He has been bred
in the slums that a totalitarian plutocracy had ignored,
and now his race of barbarians, with their brute ability
to survive, has become dominant. The Chauffeur has
caught and subdued Vesta Van Warden, the beautiful
widow of a man who was one of the richest and most
powerful of the plutocrats. Vesta is the mother of the
Chauffeur's one-year-old child. In what the Chauffeur

calls "a regular Garden-of-Eden proposition," his plan
is "to start all over and replenish the earth and multi-
ply." At the conclusion of the story, Smith is an old man
called "Granser," who reflects on the destruction of his
own civilization and "the flood of primordial life" that
replaced it. London once again tried to play down the
phantasmic qualities of the novel, referring to it as
merely a "pseudo-scientific story."[12] But the dreamlike
ending in which London pours forth a crescendo of
images involving the foamy sea, wild horses, screaming
cougars, and bellowing sea lions as Smith disappears
into the forest is horrifyingly apocalyptic.

London was a great admirer of Poe, and the situation that generates the story line of *The Scarlet Plague*
derives from Poe's "The Masque of the Red Death." In
"The Tragic and Terrible in Fiction," London stated his
own affinity to Poe, and also provided an excellent indi-
rect commentary on what makes *The Scarlet Plague* so
psychologically chilling, by asking, "What is it that
sends the heart fluttering up and quickens the feet of
the man or woman who goes alone down a dark hall or
up a winding stair? Is it a stirring of the savage in
them? — of the savage who has slept, but never died,
since the time the river-folk crouched over the fires of
their squatting places, or the tree-folk bunched together and chattered in the dark?" London then an-
swers his own questions: "Whatever the thing is, and
whether it be good or evil, it is a thing and it is real. It
is the thing Poe rouses in us, scaring us in broad day
and throwing us into 'admired disorders.'"[13]

London's most extensive analysis of these disorders is found in *The Star Rover*, which is structured
around the memoir of Ed Morrell, an ex-convict and a
frequent guest at London's ranch in 1911. Morrell remembered London as a man who thrived on fantasy
and who once entered into an imaginary conspiracy
with Morrell to steal the state of Arizona by establish-

ing a political machine that would take over the state government. Morrell had endured five years of solitary confinement while at Folsom and San Quentin prisons, much of the time laced into a straitjacket. London was fascinated by Morrell's account of surviving the agonies of the jacket through a form of self-hypnosis that made it possible for him to become a "star rover" and travel back through time and space to previous lives. London entered into an agreement with Morrell over dinner at the Saddle Rock Restaurant in Oakland in December 1911 to use Morrell's recollections in a novel attacking the American prison system. His description of jail conditions in the first third of the novel is in the form of an exposé, but the remainder of the novel turns into a wild extrapolation of Morrell's fanciful flights into the lives lived by his former selves.

Morrell figures as an actual character, along with Jake Oppenheimer, a friend of Morrell's at San Quentin who was sentenced to death for striking a guard. One of the reasons London wrote the novel was to get the statute that applied to Oppenheimer's case revoked (it was, but not before Oppenheimer was executed). Oppenheimer and Morrell, who have devised a system of communication involving knuckle-rapping, are joined in solitary by Darrell Standing, who had been a professor of agronomics at California-Davis, and who was given a life sentence for killing another academic. He is sent to the solitary cells because the warden believes Standing has hidden dynamite somewhere within the prison. The warden tries to break Standing by having him laced into a straitjacket ever tighter, for ever longer periods. Although the book is intended as an accurate depiction of prison life, it actually comes to center on what London termed its "key-note": the triumph of the spirit.[14] Standing maintains that "matter is the only illusion," and his astral-projection trips soon make the warden's desperate sadism seem insignificant.

Believing he has "lived millions of years" and has "possessed many bodies," Standing masters the art of transporting himself back into his earlier existences, and the accounts of his travels make the novel into a series of fragmented collages. Standing tells of his former lives as a dashing French count given to swordplay during the late Renaissance, an American youth who is killed by Mormons and Indians at the Mountain Meadow Massacre in 1860, a fourth-century Christian monk living in an Egyptian cave, an English sailor who fights in sixteenth-century Korea and marries a Korean princess, a Danish Viking who becomes a Roman soldier under Pontius Pilate, a resourceful castaway who lives alone on a desert island for eight years in the nineteenth century, and finally a caveman at the dawn of human consciousness. Unfortunately, these stories are ones London had been contemplating as entire novels in themselves but could never quite work out as self-sustaining narratives.

In her criticism of *The Star Rover*, Joan London pointed out that it "was Jack's last attempt at serious work. Into this extraordinary and little-known book he flung with a prodigal hand riches that he had hoarded for years, and compressed into brilliant episodes notes originally intended for full-length books."[15] It is as if the novel is an unburdening of unresolved potentialities in a way that is as often lyrically inspired as it is poorly motivated. London described *The Star Rover* as "a book that cuts various ways" in that while the prison conditions are gruesome, the story itself is not. London saw an essential optimism in the victim's ability to escape the tortures of the jacket "to win love, adventure, romance, and the life everlasting."[16]

London, in his self-estimate, was a thoroughgoing materialist, but, as *The Star Rover* attests, he was always open to questions concerning the other side of reality. He grew up in a household where levitation was an ordinary occurrence and where the spirits of Indian chiefs sat down to powwow at his mother's séances. In his own fantastic business schemes, London sometimes acted as if time and distance did not exist, as if he would have an eternity for everything he wanted to do. As much as he was devoted to the pleasures of raw-beef sandwiches, his stories offer repeated instances in which such characters as the Malemute Kid and Darrell Standing demonstrate the superiority of mind over matter.

Despite his repeated protests, London had an imagination that was stirred by accounts of supernatural happenings; and whether or not he believed in these, at times his narrative powers were great enough to make them seem real. In *Before Adam*, *The Scarlet Plague*, and *The Star Rover*, London claimed to be playing games with his audience. London scoffed at superstition, but one of his frequent entertainments was to demonstrate magic tricks for his quests. Perhaps he was more like the old Klondiker from one of his early stories than he was willing to admit, a man "who believed in omens and thought-transference," and who "deemed these dream-robbers to be the astral projection of real personages who happened at those particular moments, no matter where they were in the flesh, to be harboring designs, in the spirit, upon his wealth."[17]

Jack London was spooked by a lot of things out of his childhood, but, whatever his repressed superstitions might have been, the Jack London most of us want to know is the devoted sportsman and adventurer who loved sailing, fishing, duck hunting, bicycling, and boxing. So long as his health stood up, London was willing to put the gloves on with anyone, and he was a sports nut throughout his life. When he stopped in Hawaii with the *Snark*, he did an amazing thing for the times: he learned how to surf with one of the few Ha-

waiians who was still practicing the sport. London was
therefore one of the first Californians to become an
expert in what was to become his home state's most
favored pastime. He enjoyed having fun — a rare trait
among American writers — and at the end of his working day at his ranch, he liked to set time aside for
riding, swimming, wrestling, or boxing with his friends.
London's interest in sports shows up in his writing
again and again, and much of his popularity during his
lifetime can be attributed to the credibility he established as an authority on the American sporting scene.

London occasionally worked as a sportswriter for
the San Francisco *Examiner*, and his career as a reporter
began early and led to a series of memorable articles, as
well as four works of sports fiction: the novels *The Game*
(1905) and *The Abysmal Brute* (1913), and the stories "A
Piece of Steak" (1909) and "The Mexican" (1910). On
the basis of his Klondike adventures and stories, London was hired by the *Examiner* in 1901, and he wrote
seventeen articles during his first year, including ten
insightful pieces on a shooting festival and one on the
James J. Jeffries and Gus Ruhlin fight that took place
in San Francisco on November 16, 1901. In revealing
that London would be working for the paper, the editors of the *Examiner* made the announcement on July 13
that London would "write in his own graphic style what
he has seen."

The Third National Bundes Shooting Festival, or
"Schützenfest," began in San Francisco on July 15 at
Shell Mound Park, involving sharpshooters of German
descent from shooting clubs across the country and
some from Germany. London's first article includes a
description of the opening parade and mentions how
"the great crowd scattered . . . in quest of the national
beverage that made Milwaukee famous."[18] The following articles are full of vivid details on how the riflemen
prepare for competition, the variety of sights and rests
they employ, and why most of them prefer the 32-40

Pope target rifle. London records the scores of the top competitors, telling how "Jacob Meyer of the Sacramento Helvetia Schützen made the best 71 out of a possible 80 on the ring target," but most of his column inches are given to knowledgeable explanations of technique, speculations on the value of riflemen in modern warfare, and a study of the "exalted condition" the best competitors work themselves into while concentrating on the target. Not content with describing events from the firing positions, London spent a day in the target pits, and in all of the articles London's eye for a story is apparent, even on days when nothing of unusual interest was going on.

In his report of the Jeffries–Ruhlin fight, London displays the same genius for getting at the action beyond the action. Jeffries dominated Ruhlin, and the fight ended with Ruhlin's seconds literally throwing in the sponge. London, with his great eye for just the right image, writes of how "the blood, conveyed by the gloves, marked lightly the bodies of both men with crimson splashes." But much of the article details the crowd's reaction, the "sea of faces" with the "house in darkness and the ring a white blaze of light." London pauses to comment on his own response: "And under this veneer of a thousand years of culture, I, for one, found the endless savage centuries still lived. I who had come to note the blood cry of the crowd, came to myself with sickening consciousness to find that my voice, too, was issuing forth with lusty joy and thrilling abandon." All of London's subsequent boxing stories show his appreciation for the sport, and he was quick to defend it against its detractors. In "The Somnambulists" (*Revolution and Other Essays*), he justifies boxing in another way: "Far better to have the front of one's face pushed in by the fist of an honest prize fighter than to have the lining of one's stomach corroded by the embalmed beef of a dishonest manufacturer."

London shows the natural sportswriter's ability to

see the "theme" in each event and, while highly descriptive, his articles usually move toward an analysis of what is at stake as two men confront each other in the ring. A good example is his coverage of the Jimmy Britt–Battling Nelson bout at Colma, California, on September 10, 1905. The two fighters are opposites. Nelson is "a fighting animal," while Britt is an "intelligent animal." Nelson, the "lower type," wins the fight in the eighteenth round. London reports what happened, but then he steps aside to reflect on what it means. He sees Nelson as an "abysmal brute" and explains that Britt lost because he is the "higher type," not as callous to pain and shock as was Nelson. "Britt was knocked out because his body was not strong enough to keep his mind poised in control and directing his body," London writes. "When the body was weakened the mind was overthrown, and his intelligence counted for nothing."

London saw the boxing ring as an emblem of his Darwinism, and his atavistic fears are apparent in every boxing story he wrote. Although this conception of the sport is now a cliché, London was one of the sportswriters who established it. He captures the appeal of our most primitive sport because he saw represented in it both the best and the worst in human nature. Part of his enthusiasm, of course, is that of the true fan—the one who wishes he were good enough to be in there himself. Here is London's concluding paragraph on the Britt–Nelson fight: "Nevertheless all hail to both of them! They play the clean game of life. And I, for one, would rather be either of them this day at Colma than a man who took no exercise with his body to-day but instead waxed physically gross in the course of gathering to himself a few dollars in the commercial game."

London's most famous boxing articles are those he wrote about the great black fighter Jack Johnson. London covered Johnson's fight with Tommy Burns in Sydney, Australia, on December 27, 1908, and also John son's fight with Jeffries at Reno, Nevada, on July 4, 1910. London has long been accused of blatant racism in his treatment of Johnson, but the truth is that London developed a great admiration for Johnson's skills, and described the fighter as the man with the "golden smile." At a time when Johnson's love of big cars and beautiful women was offensive to most Americans, London wrote about the glamour of a man who is now regarded by some as the greatest of all heavyweight champions. Like other sportswriters of the time, London did get caught up on the "great white hope" idea that both the hapless Burns and the aging Jeffries represented. But London states his original position calmly and reasonably: "Personally, I was with Burns all the way. He is a white man, and so am I. Naturally I wanted to see the white man win. Put the case to Johnson and ask him if he were the spectator at a fight between a white man and a black man which he would like to see win. Johnson's black skin will dictate a desire parallel to the one dictated by my white skin." But London follows this by writing, "Jack Johnson, here's my hand, too. I wanted to see the other fellow win, but you were the best man. Shake." London was also instrumental in setting up what was to become the first and best of dozens of "fights of the century," when he ended his dispatch by writing that "Jeffries must emerge from his alfalfa farm and wipe that smile from Johnson's face," which is just what Jeffries tried to do a year-and-a-half later in Reno.

London went to Reno on assignment from the New York *Herald* and wrote daily articles beginning on June 23. Among other things, these articles are valuable accounts of life in Reno and what London calls its "gambling hazards" before it became the vacation spot it is today; and he has the inadvertently prophetic line, "There are easier ways of spending money than by traveling all the way to Reno." When Johnson arrived on

June 24, London was waiting for him: "His voice was just as jovial, his handshake as hearty, his smile as dazzling as when I last saw him in Australia." To London, Johnson is a man who "cannot hold a grudge," and while Jeffries is a "fighter," Johnson is a "boxer."

In his June 26 article, London displays his knowledge of boxing in a commentary on the merits of each fighter in reference to Gentleman Jim Corbett and Jack Sharkey, concluding that Johnson has the edge but that he will have to "put up the fight of his life." And in his best buildup article, telegraphed on June 28, London begins with the kind of lead every sportswriter dreams of writing: "Here is the problem. At 1:30 o'clock in the afternoon of July 4 two men, a white and a black, are going to face each other in a squared ring, elevated in the centre of a large arena. They are not going to try to kill each other." As it turned out, it was not much of a battle. Twenty thousand people, lured by the legendary promoter Tex Rickard, watched Corbett try to unnerve Johnson by taunting him from Jeffries' corner. From the fifth round on, Jeffries' face was not free of blood, and every remark Corbett made resulted in more punishment for him, until Johnson finally put him down for good in the fifteenth round. It was the first time Jeffries had been knocked out. To London, Johnson was "this amazing negro from Texas, this black man with the unfailing smile, this king of fighters and monologists." London wrote this when the hostility toward Johnson was so great that some newspapers did not want to acknowledge his victory at all and downplayed his superb mastery of Jeffries. The fight was proclaimed as a racial war, but London was one of the few reporters who was willing to state his open admiration for Jack Johnson the man and the athlete.

London's involvement as a spectator at boxing matches was said to be so intense that no one wanted to sit next to him. His thorough understanding of the

sport led to some sports fiction that established patterns
for the genre, and he was one of the first writers to take
sports seriously as the raw material for novels and stories. He was also one of the first to deliberately avoid
the exaggerated use of sports slang that was epidemic among the sports journalists of his era and that later
carried into the work of Damon Runyon, Ring
Lardner, and Heywood Broun when they turned to
fiction.

London's sports fiction has the same strengths that
his sportswriting does: vivid imagery, terse, hard-hitting style, and close attention to technical details. Although London was not the first American writer to use
sporting scenes significantly in his stories, he was one
of the first to write about boxing in a way that gave the
sport respectability as a topic for serious fiction.[19] He
also set forth some of the stereotypes that persist in
boxing stories and films to this day. In *The Game*, for
instance, he writes about a boxer who is killed in the
ring after deciding to fight just one more time. In "A
Piece of Steak," London sets up the recurring plot of the
aging fighter who is beaten by a young challenger. In
"The Mexican," the hero endures the racist jibes of a
hostile crowd to defeat a gringo opponent who calls him
a "little Mexican rat." And in *The Abysmal Brute*, London
depicts a boxer who is a tough but sensitive man caught
up in a brutal sport, a man who packs a terrific knock-
out punch but who also reads Browning and Shakespeare and frequents art museums.

Part of London's genius in his sports fiction is that
he keeps his plot lines simple and lets his hero's attitude
toward his sport define his character. London's prose is
well suited to this type of story, and his style backs up
the action like a combination of body punches followed
by a stiff uppercut. London's own boxing experience
(he had been knocked out at least once) adds to the
veracity of his boxing stories, and he is simultaneously

able to capture the sweaty appeal of the sport as well as its depravity.

"He was only a boy, as she was only a girl," London writes in the opening chapter of *The Game*, establishing at once the contrast between the innocent love of curly-haired Joe Fleming and delicate Genevieve Pritchard, and the beastly "Game" in which Joe makes his living. Joe and Genevieve are natural in every sense of the word, and London explains their attraction in Darwinian terms: "His masculinity, the masculinity of the fighting male, made its inevitable appeal to her, a female, moulded by her heredity to seek out the strong man for mate and to lean against the wall of his strength." Joe wants Genevieve to watch his last fight — something of a problem because women were not allowed into the arenas at the time. Genevieve disguises herself as a boy, however, and watches the fight through a peephole in a wall.

Drawing on his memories of the Jeffries–Ruhlin fight, London represents Joe's opponent as a "beast with a streak for a forehead, with beady eyes under lowering and bushy brows, flat-nosed, thick-lipped, sullen mouthed . . . with a hairy growth that matted like a dog's on his chest and shoulders." The action is described in rapid-fire sentences, Joe getting the best of it with his superior technique. But just as he is about to bring the punishment to an end, Joe slips on the wet canvas, gets caught on the chin with a lucky punch, and, as London relates, "He went over backward. Genevieve saw his muscles relax while he was yet in the air, and she heard the thud of his head on the canvas." In his final paragraph, London comments on the concept of sport and what the idea of the Game entails, the oddly obsessive "grip it laid on men's souls, its irony and faithlessness, its risks and hazards and fierce insurgence of the blood." Although it is the sport itself that takes him from her, Genevieve sadly realizes that even if Joe had lived, he could never have been fully hers: the Game would always be his "heart's desire."

"A Piece of Steak," despite its Australian setting, is a thematic sequel to *The Game*. Tom King's life at forty is a bleak glimpse of the future that might have awaited Joe Fleming. Once champion, Tom is so broke that he can barely feed his family, much less buy the steak he needs to get his strength up for a winner-take-all fight with a younger opponent named Sandel. Tom sadly reflects, as he walks down the aisle to enter the ring, that most of the men in the audience were "kiddies" when he won his first fight.

Sandel is fast, but Tom's wiliness prevails until the eleventh round, when he knocks Sandel to the canvas. The younger man's endurance saves him, and he struggles to his feet at the count of nine. Tom is finished; he does not have the strength for the final punch that would finish off Sandel. "Tom King's bleared eyes saw the gloved fist driving at his jaw, and he willed to guard it by interposing his arm," London writes in a passage that is typical of his action scenes. "He saw the danger, willed the act; but the arm was too heavy. It seemed burdened with a hundred weight of lead. It would not lift itself, and he strove to lift it with his soul. Then the gloved fist landed home. He experienced a sharp snap that was like an electric spark, and, simultaneously, the veil of blackness enveloped him."

In "The Mexican" London develops a theme that has since become a sports cliché: the idea that boxing is one of the few paths to money for members of certain minority groups in a white society. Felipe Rivera, a young Mexican fighter who has pledged all of his earnings to the Junta opposing Díaz in the Revolution, is a last-minute replacement on a fight card with the great Danny Ward. Determined to get at least five thousand dollars to buy weapons for the Revolution, Rivera challenges Ward to fight on a no-split deal. Ward, with his experience and superior size, agrees, warning Rivera that he will beat him to death in the ring. But Rivera is able to last until the seventeenth round, when a clean drive to Ward's mouth, followed by a "down-chop of the right on neck and jaw," fells the favorite. There are no congratulations from the crowd, but Rivera, leaning backward on the ropes in his corner and glaring hatred at the ten thousand gringos in the crowd, remembers that "The guns were his. The Revolution could go on."

London was under no illusions concerning the nature of boxing as a business, and much of the story centers on the corruption of the sport and how Rivera must understand that the fight is intended to boost Ward's reputation for an upcoming championship bout. Rivera is told to try to last at least until the twelfth round, and when it becomes shockingly apparent that he has a chance at winning, the promoter insists that Rivera take a dive.

Although not nearly as effective as a documentary piece, *The Abysmal Brute* takes a somewhat similar approach to boxing as an enterprise. Pat Glendon — "a creature of the wild, more a night-roaming figure from some old fairy story or folk tale than a twentieth-century youth" — emerges from the mountains to knock out every ranking heavyweight on natural ability alone; and in a manner oddly prophetic of Muhammad Ali even calls his fights in advance. He meets Maud Sangster, newspaper reporter, poet, and state tennis champion, who convinces him that he should get out of boxing while he still can. In a narratively bizarre ending, Pat begins his last fight with a long speech to the crowd in which he talks about the evils of capitalism and the corruption he has witnessed in the boxing world. The result is a riot, which Pat resolves by knocking out *both* his opponent and the ex-heavyweight champion, who tries to intervene, with single blows. Pat and Maud then retire to his beloved mountains, returning to the innocence of nature, where Pat is anything but an abysmal beast.

When the novel came out, one commentator concisely set forth both its merits and London's main virtue as a writer of sports fiction: "In his own picturesque Western style Jack London hustles the reader through the whole process of preparing for the winning of a world's heavyweight championship. And when you have finished reading through *The Abysmal Brute*, you will realize that the soul of prizefighting, with all its gallantry and sordidness, its heroic points and drab grossness has been laid bare."[20] The thud of the blows, the finagling of the managers, promoters, and fighters behind the scenes, the mood of the crowd, as well as the smells of the beer-soaked arenas — all of this is captured in London's boxing stories. And his work, in addition to establishing certain narrative patterns in the genre of sports fiction, had some impact on cleaning the sport up and making it possible for Jack Dempsy, Gene Tunney, and other boxers to enjoy the worshipful respect they received at the height of their careers a decade or so later. London's sports fiction was also well received by some fighters themselves, and it is said that it was Tunney's reading of *The Game* that made him decide on his retirement. Later on, Tunney supposedly gave Rocky Marciano a copy of the book, and encouraged him to make a timely decision on quitting the ring.[21]

London, of course, used the sport of boxing to illustrate some of his pet theories concerning man's essential animal nature and saw fighting as an instinctive urge deriving from "the ape and tiger in us," but there is the boyish enthusiasm of the true fan running through virtually every sentence he wrote about sports. He probably meant it when he said in 1910, "I would rather be heavyweight champion of the world — which I never can be — than King of England, or President of the United States, or Kaiser of Germany."[22]

In another remark made during his last years, London said he "would rather be a superb meteor, every atom of me in magnificent glow, than a sleepy and permanent planet. The proper function of man is to live, not to exist."[23] London's fervor for life is reflected in many ways, but perhaps no better than in the sheer variety of his writing. He believed that a professional writer should be able to take the world as his literary province, and London himself very nearly did so.

It is a mistake to assume that at the end of his daily stint he simply set his writing aside. His extensive reading and traveling continually brought new topics to mind, and at the end of his life his proposed projects ranged from a study of Asian agricultural practices to an account of his experiences with women that would be so candid it could be published only under a pseudonym or anonymously. Unlike many writers of fiction, London did not have an exaggerated opinion of himself as some sort of shaman or magical storyteller. He preferred to think of himself as a working-class writer, and his willingness simply to turn his pen to the job at hand and do the best he could — whether it meant detailing the sufferings of the lepers on Molokai or praising the superb skills of Jack Johnson — makes reading his obscure and unusual pieces surprisingly satisfying. However pressured he might have been in writing his lesser-known work, such as his *Examiner* articles, London tried to give good value for the money he received — and most of the time he did.

6

Crowbar in Hand

"Atmosphere stands always for the elimination of the artist, that is to say, the atmosphere is the artist," London wrote in 1900.[1] This is a principle London demonstrated in the good strong phrases of his distinctively straightforward style. But as much as he wanted to inject life and movement into his work through his self-effacing mastery of the writer's trade, his readers have never been willing to put up with the willful elimination of London from his own books. Behind everything he wrote looms a strong personality who represents, in most respects, all that is good in a life of fierce adventure and intensive study. Much of his writing is wild and savage, and he had huge appetites that eventually wore down what was once a powerful constitution. His life was one of enormous private struggle, and if it ended too suddenly, too sadly, it was because of the very fault that contributed so greatly to his success: he wanted too much, and he wanted it all at once. But as hard as he drove himself to succeed in the literary marketplace, as much as he tended to see his own existence as the survival of the fittest, he produced a body of writing that is striking not so much for its quantity as for its enduring potency.

For a long time, London was regarded as a fascinating but seriously flawed writer, one given to shallow intellectualism and racial prejudices, at best the popularizer of outdated ideas, at worst the representative of dangerous political tendencies. This is the Jack London portrayed in many of the scholarly attempts at documenting and analyzing American culture in the early decades of this century. In *The American Mind*, for instance, the historian Henry Steele Commager sees London as an enthusiastic but naive writer who used science and philosophy for the purposes of conspiracy. "London translated Darwinism into the vernacular, presented it in a guise so romantic, boisterous, and extravagant that it proved irresistible," Commager intones; "he wrote it up in dime novels and purveyed it as literature and philosophy. The stuff of his endless adventure stories was dredged up from his own fabulous career as newsboy, oyster pirate, tramp, sailor, prospector, and rancher; the philosophy was laid on like ornamental scrollwork on Eastlake buildings."[2]

London was indeed a translator of ideas, and he was to a large extent a propagandist in his work; but he was not insincere in doing this, and it is wrong to regard the socialist doctrines voiced in *The Iron Heel* and *Martin Eden* as ornamentation. London used his fiction as a way of popularizing his beliefs, and if the "living philosophy" he sometimes has such characters as Ernest Everhard spout seems rough and intrusive, that is just the way London wanted it to be. He was preaching revolution when he wrote those books, and the revolution he envisioned would be rough, raw, and mean. At the height of his socialist frenzies, London comes across as something of a cultural primitive, and in his conception of himself as a revolutionist it is as if he were trying a little too hard to live out a proletarian fiction of himself. But as an advocate of social change, he demanded to be taken seriously, and he meant it when he said that as a socialist he was "content to labor, crowbar in hand, shoulder to shoulder with intellectuals, idealists, and class-conscious workingmen, getting a solid pry now and again and setting the whole edifice rocking. Some day, when we get a few more hands and crowbars to work, we'll topple it over, along with all its rotten life and unburied dead, its monstrous selfishness and sodden materialism."[3]

London's socialism is now a long-lost cause in America, but behind his vision, despite his tendency toward violence-stained rhetoric, is a concept of literature as a means of impelling his audience to action in achieving "a new habitation for mankind, in which there will be no parlor floor, in which all the rooms will be bright and airy, and where the air that is breathed will be clean, noble, and alive."[4]

At his greatest, Darwinist and materialist though he was, London wrote with an intense presence of purpose. He realized the importance, as Philip José Farmer puts it, "of telling a story as if it were fuel for a fire."[5] He said he wanted to live a hundred years, not to pile up money, but to learn what impact his writing would have. "See the boxes of notes filed away?" he asked his wife. "Why, writers I know are looking about for plots, and I've enough here to keep me busy with twice a hundred novels."[6] These were to be books that would change things for the better, London believed. We are all worse off that they were never written.

"Dealing only with the artist, be it understood, only those artists will go down who have spoken true of us," said London, regarding literary immortality. "Their truth must be the deepest and most significant, their voices clear and strong, definite and coherent."[7] This is what London has given us with his complex intermingling of experience and ideas, and his influence on his readers has always been immediate and sometimes oddly dramatic, even in some of his worst work. One of his purposes in writing his last dog story, *Michael, Brother of Jerry*, was to protest the cruel methods used in training animals for the vaudeville stage. In his preface, London suggested that clubs be formed to deal with the problem of exploited animals. Thousands of readers responded by walking out of theaters whenever such acts were presented. By 1924, the Jack London clubs had a worldwide membership of four hundred thousand, and the tightrope-walking dogs and dancing bears had all but disappeared from vaudeville shows in the United States.[8] An extreme example, perhaps, but London's work remains forceful, capable of living on its own long after it has been put down. He offers a fierce combination of bold thought and compellingly intense language because he had faith in a culture far beyond the one he lived in. And he was committed to one overriding resolve: to "create things that live, and breathe, and grip men, and cause reading lamps to burn overtime."[9]

Notes

1. THE BRAIN MERCHANT

1. Jack London to George Sterling, October 31, 1908, *Letters from Jack London*, ed. King Hendricks and Irving Shepard (New York: Odyssey Press, 1965), p. 272.
2. Andrew Sinclair, *Jack: A Biography of Jack London* (New York: Pocket Books, 1979), p. 190.
3. Cited by Russ Kingman, *A Pictorial Life of Jack London* (New York: Crown, 1979), p.126.
4. Cited by Sinclair, pp. 243-44.
5. Ford Madox Ford (Oliver Madox Hueffer), "Jack London, A Personal Sketch,"in *Critical Essays on Jack London*, ed. Jacqueline Tavernier-Courbin(Boston : G. K. Hall, 1983), p. 31.
6. For a useful analysis of the London biographies, see Richard W. Etulain, "The Lives of Jack London," in *Critical Essays on Jack London*, pp. 43-56. For another treatment of the subject, see Clarice Stasz, "The Social Construction of Biography: The Case of Jack London," *Modern Fiction Studies* 22 (1976): 51-71.
7. Cited by Kingman, p. 77.
8. Cited by Kingman, p. 164.
9. Cited by Kingman, p. 20.
10. Kevin Starr, *Americans and the California Dream, 1850-1915* (New York: Oxford University Press, 1973), p. 240.
11. Jack London, *The Little Lady of the Big House* (New York: Macmillan, 1916), p. 49.
12. Joan London, *Jack London and His Times* (Seattle: University of Washington Press, 1968), p. 1.
13. *The George Eliot Letters*, ed. Gordon Haight (New Haven: Yale University Press, 1954-55), 5:252-53.
14. Robert Barltrop, *Jack London: The Man, the Writer, the Rebel* (London: Pluto Press, 1976), p. 15.

15. Joan London, p. 11.
16. Jack London, *John Barleycorn* (New York: Century, 1913), p. 18.
17. Joan London, p. 22.
18. Ouida, *Signa* (New York: Peter Fenelon Collier, n.d.), p. 8.
19. George Wharton James, "A Study of Jack London in His Prime," *Overland Monthly* 69 (May 1917): 368.
20. This point is made by Alfred Kazin, *On Native Grounds: An Interpretation of Modern American Prose Literature* (New York: Harcourt Brace, 1942), p. 111.
21. Sinclair, p. 13.
22. San Francisco *Morning Call*, November 12, 1893.
23. Joan London, pp. 66–67.
24. Joan London, pp. 77–78.
25. On this point, see Joan London, p. 134.
26. Jack London, "First Aid to Rising Authors," in *No Mentor but Myself: A Collection of Articles, Essays, Reviews, and Letters*, ed. Dale L. Walker (Port Washington, N.Y.: Kennikat, 1979), p. 28.
27. Cited by Joan London, p. 146.
28. Edward E. P. Morgan, *God's Loaded Dice* (Caldwell, Idaho: Caxton Printers, 1948), p. 127.
29. For a brief account of this expedition, see Kingman, p. 78.
30. Jack London, "Getting into Print," in *No Mentor but Myself*, p. 55.
31. Cited by Kingman, p. 94.
32. Frederick Jackson Turner, *The Frontier in American History* (New York: Scribners, 1920), p. 2.
33. Theodore Roosevelt, *The Winning of the West: The Works of Theodore Roosevelt* (New York: H. Holt, 1924–26), 10:101–2.
34. Cited by Barltrop, p. 71.
35. Joan London, p. 204.
36. Cited by Sinclair, p. 60.
37. Cited by Charmian London, *The Book of Jack London*, 2 vols. (New York: Century, 1921), 1:12–13.
38. Jack London to Cloudesley Johns, July 11, 1903, *Letters*, p 151.

39. Joan London, p.68.
40. Cited by Kingman, p. 159.
41. Jack London to George P. Brett, June 7, 1905, *Letters*, p. 175.
42. Jack London to George P. Brett, August 1, 1905, *Letters*, p. 177.
43. Starr, p. 228.
44. Sinclair, p. 181.
45. Cited by Sinclair, p. 241.
46. Floyd Dell, *Homecoming* (New York: Farrar Rinehart, 1933), p. 283.
47. Jack London to Ralph Kaspar, June 25, 1914, *Letters*, p. 425.
48. Philip S. Foner, *Jack London: American Rebel* (New York: The Citadel Press, 1947), p. 125.
49. For a detailed and convincing examination of the circumstances surrounding London's death, see Alfred S. Shivers, "Jack London: Not a Suicide," in *Critical Essays on Jack London*, pp. 57–69.
50. H.L. Mencken, "Jack London," in *Critical Essays on Jack London*, p. 25.
51. Charmian London, 2:323.
52. Jack London to Editor of the *Bulletin*, September 17, 1898, p. 3.

2. MEDITATIONS ON MAN AND BEAST

1. Jack London, "The Gold Hunters of the North," in *Revolution and Other Essays* (New York: Macmillan, 1910), p. 162.
2. Cited by Sinclair, p. 41.
3. Jack London, "In a Far Country," in *Novels and Stories*, The Library of America (New York: Viking, 1982), p. 308.
4. Jack London to Cloudesley Johns, April 17, 1899, *Letters*, p. 29.
5. Ibid.
6. Jack London to George P. Brett, January 30, 1902, *Letters*, p. 129.

7. Cited by Franklin Walker, *Jack London and the Klondike* (San Marino, Calif.: The Huntington Library, 1978), p. 223.

8. Jack London to George P. Brett, March 7, 1907, *Letters*, p. 241.

9. Charmian London, 1:384.

10. Jack London to Frederick H. Robinson, September 5, 1913, *Letters*, p. 398.

11. E.O. Wilson, *Sociobiology: The New Synthesis* (Cambridge, Mass.: Harvard University Press, 1975), p. 41.

12. Reprinted as "Men Who Misinterpret Nature," in *The Works of Theodore Roosevelt*, p. 4.

13. L. David Mech, *The Wolf* (Garden City, N.Y.: Natural History Press, 1970), p. 291.

14. Barry Lopez, *Of Wolves and Men* (New York: Scribners, 1978), p. 218.

15. "Literary Table: Glimpses of New Books," *Current Literature* 35 (July–Dec. 1903):369.

16. "Fiction," *Critic* 43 (July–Dec. 1903):582.

17. Jack London to George P. Brett, February 18, 1915, *Letters*, pp. 449–50.

18. Cited by Joan London, p. 252.

19. George Jean Nathan, *The Theatre Book of the Year, 1942–43* (New York: Knopf, 1943), p. 68.

20. Jack London to George P. Brett, December 5, 1904, *Letters*, p. 166.

21. *The Independent* 61 (July–Dec. 1906): 1055–56.

22. *The Nation* 83 (July–Dec. 1906):440–41.

23. *The Forum* 38 (July–June 1906–7):549.

24. Kazin, p. 87.

3. SUPERMAN AND THE SOCIAL PIT

1. Cited by Sinclair, p. 167.

2. Jack London to Mr. Ricks, August 17, 1911, *Letters*, p. 350.

3. Jack London, "Introduction to *The Cry for Justice*," in *No Mentor but Myself*, p. 155.

4. See Joan London, pp. 210–14.

5. Joan London, p. 211.
6. Jack London to Cloudesley Johns, July 5, 1899, *Letters*, p. 43.
7. Cited by Joan London, pp. 212–13.
8. Jack London to Members, Local Glen Ellen, Socialist Labor Party, March 7, 1916, *Letters*, p. 467.
9. "Nietzsche in England," *The Nation* 96 (Jan.–June 1913):590.
10. Jack London to Mary Austin, November 5, 1915, *Letters*, p. 463.
11. Jack London to Carrie Sterling, September 15, 1905, *Letters*, p. 180.
12. Cited by Kingman, pp. 125–26.
13. Charmian London, 2:57.
14. For more on this point, see Joan London, p. 305.
15. Foner, pp. 72–73.
16. George Orwell to Rev. H. Rogers, 1946, *Collected Essays, Journalism, and Letters of George Orwell*, ed. Sonia Orwell and Ian Angus (New York: Harcourt Brace and World, 1968), p. 4.
17. Cited by Foner, p. 96.
18. Foner, p. 97.
19. San Francisco *Chronicle*, December 21, 1905, p. 2.
20. Cited by Foner, p. 59.
21. Conway Zirkle, *Evolution, Marxism, Biology, and the Social Scene* (Philadelphia: University of Pennsylvania Press, 1959), pp. 318–37.
22. Cited by Foner, p. 67.

4. THE NAKED FACTS OF LIFE

1. Jack London to Lorrin Thurston, June 11,1910, *Letters*, p. 311.
2. Jack London to George Sterling, March 3, 1909, *Letters*, p. 277.
3. Jack London to the Rev. Charles Brown, Open Letter, June 1910, *Letters*, p. 307.
4. Jack London to Roland Phillips, February 27, 1913, *Letters*, p. 372.

5. Alfred Kazin, "The Self as History: Reflections on Autobiography," in *The American Autobiography*, ed. Albert E. Stone (Englewood Cliffs, N.J.: Prentice Hall, 1981), p. 35.

6. Jack London to George P. Brett, March 7, 1907, *Letters*, p. 241.

7. *Independent* 64 (Jan.–June 1908):42.

8. Jack London to George Sterling, February 17, 1908, *Letters*, p. 257.

9. Henry James, *The Art of the Novel*, ed. R.P. Blackmur (New York: Scribners, 1934), p. 4.

10. Jack London to the Rev. Charles Brown, Open Letter, June 1910, *Letters*, p. 307.

11. Jack London to Mary Banks Krasky, December 12, 1914, *Letters*, pp. 439–40.

12. "Recent Fiction and the Critics," *Current Literature* 47 (July–Dec. 1909):695.

13. Jack London to Cloudesley Johns, February 17, 1908, *Letters*, p. 257.

14. Jack London to Wm. W. Ellsworth, September 7, 1912, *Letters*, p. 363.

15. Sinclair, p. 191.

16. Charmian London, 2:245.

17. Jack London to Wm. W. Ellsworth, January 30, 1913, *Letters*, p. 369.

18. *The Nation* 97 (July–Dec. 1913):190.

19. New York *Times*, November 3, 1915, p. 1.

20. Jack London to T.A. Bostick, September 28, 1913, *Letters*, p. 401.

21. Jack London to George P. Brett, July 11, 1907, *Letters*, p. 245.

5. WORKING-CLASS WRITER

1. Jack London to Miss Esther Andersen, December 11, 1914, *Letters*, p. 437.

2. Marcus Cunliffe, *The Literature of the United States* (Baltimore: Penguin, 1970), p. 220.

3. Jack London, "Again the Literary Aspirant," in *No Mentor but Myself*, p. 48.

4. For an excellent account of this phase of London's career, see Earle Labor, "Jack London's Pacific World," in *Critical Essays on Jack London*, pp. 205-22.

5. Jack London, *The Cruise of the Snark* (New York: Macmillan, 1911), pp. 5-6.

6. *The Cruise of the Snark*, p. 59.

7. *Jack London: A Biography* (Boston: Little, Brown, 1964), p. 220.

8. Jack London to Joseph Conrad, January 4, 1915, *Letters*, p. 451.

9. Jack London to Roland Phillips, March 26, 1914, *Letters*, p. 418.

10. Jack London to C.F. Lowrie, January 13, 1911, *Letters*, p. 332.

11. Loren Eiseley, "Jack London, Evolutionist," epilogue to Jack London, *Before Adam* (New York: Macmillan, 1962), pp. 147-48.

12. Jack London to George P. Brett, April 1, 1910, *Letters*, p. 301.

13. Jack London, "The Tragic and Terrible in Fiction," in *No Mentor but Myself*, p. 61.

14. Jack London to Roland Phillips, March 26, 1914, *Letters*, p. 419.

15. Joan London, p. 362.

16. Jack London to Roland Phillips, March 26, 1914, *Letters*, p. 418.

17. Jack London, "The Man with the Gash," in *The God of His Fathers and Other Stories* (New York: McClure, Phillips, 1901), p. 118.

18. Jack London, "Schützenfest No. 1," in *Jack London Reports: War Correspondence, Sports Articles, and Miscellaneous Writings*, ed. King Hendricks and Irving Shepard (Garden City, N.Y.: Doubleday, 1970), p. 217. All subsequent sportswriting quotations come from this source.

19. For an authoritative and highly entertaining treatment of American sports fiction, with considerable emphasis on Jack London, see Michael Oriard, *Dreaming of Heroes* (Chicago: Nelson Hall, 1982).

20. Cited by Kingman, p. 225.
21. Ibid.
22. Medford *Sun*, August 18, 1911, cited by Kingman, p. 226.
23. Cited by Joan London, p. 372.

6. CROWBAR IN HAND

1. Jack London to Cloudesley Johns, June 16, 1900, *Letters*, p. 108.
2. Henry Steele Commager, *The American Mind: An Interpretation of American Thought and Character Since the 1880's* (New Haven, Conn.: Yale University Press, 1950), p. 110.
3. Jack London, "What Life Means to Me," in *No Mentor but Myself*, p. 94.
4. Ibid.
5. Philip José Farmer, Foreword to *Curious Fragments: Jack London's Tales of Fantasy Fiction*, ed. Dale L. Walker (Port Washington, N.Y.: Kennikat, 1975), p. vii.
6. Cited by Charmian London, 2:378.
7. Jack London, "These Bones Shall Rise Again," in *No Mentor but Myself*, p. 67.
8. Joan London, p. 363.
9. Jack London to Cloudesley Johns, June 16, 1900, *Letters*, p. 108.

Bibliography

I. WORKS BY JACK LONDON

Novels

The Cruise of the Dazzler. New York: Century, 1902.
A Daughter of the Snows. Philadelphia: J.B. Lippincott, 1902.
The Kempton-Wace Letters. New York: Macmillan, 1903.
The Call of the Wild. New York: Macmillan, 1903.
The Sea-Wolf. New York: Macmillan, 1904.
The Game. New York: Macmillan, 1905.
White Fang. New York: Macmillan, 1906.
Before Adam. New York: Macmillan, 1907.
The Iron Heel. New York: Macmillan, 1908.
Martin Eden. New York: Macmillan, 1909.
Burning Daylight. New York: Macmillan, 1910.
Adventure. New York: Macmillan, 1911.
The Abysmal Brute. New York: Century, 1913.
The Valley of the Moon. New York: Macmillan, 1913.
The Mutiny of the Elsinore. New York: Macmillan, 1914.
The Scarlet Plague. New York: Macmillan, 1915.
The Star Rover. New York: Macmillan, 1915.
The Little Lady of the Big House. New York: Macmillan, 1916.
Jerry of the Islands. New York: Macmillan, 1917.
Michael, Brother of Jerry. New York: Macmillan, 1917.
Hearts of Three. New York: Macmillan, 1920.
The Assassination Bureau, Ltd. New York: McGraw-Hill, 1963.
    Completed by Robert L. Fish.

Short Stories

The Son of the Wolf: Tales of the Far North. Boston: Houghton
    Mifflin, 1900.

The God of His Fathers and Other Stories. New York: McClure, Phillips, 1901.
Children of the Frost. New York: Macmillan, 1902.
The Faith of Men and Other Stories. New York: Macmillan, 1904.
Tales of the Fish Patrol. New York: Macmillan, 1905.
Moon-Face and Other Stories. New York: Macmillan, 1906.
Love of Life and Other Stories. New York: Macmillan, 1907.
Lost Face. New York: Macmillan, 1910.
When God Laughs and Other Stories. New York: Macmillan, 1911.
South Sea Tales. New York: Macmillan, 1911.
The House of Pride and Other Tales of Hawaii. New York: Macmillan, 1912.
A Son of the Sun. Garden City, N.Y.: Doubleday, Page, 1912.
Smoke Bellew. New York: Century, 1912.
The Night-Born. New York: Century, 1913.
The Strength of the Strong. New York: Macmillan, 1914.
The Turtles of Tasman. New York: Macmillan, 1916.
The Red One. New York: Macmillan, 1918.
On the Makaloa Mat. New York: Macmillan, 1919.
Dutch Courage and Other Stories. New York: Macmillan, 1922.

Essays and Travel Sketches

The People of the Abyss. New York: Macmillan, 1903.
War of the Classes. New York: Macmillan, 1905.
Revolution and Other Essays. New York: Macmillan, 1910.
The Cruise of the Snark. New York: Macmillan, 1911.
The Human Drift. New York: Macmillan, 1917.

Plays

Scorn of Women. New York: Macmillan, 1906.
Theft. New York: Macmillan, 1910.
The Acorn-Planter: A California Forest Play. New York: Macmillan, 1916.
Daughters of the Rich. Edited by James E. Sisson. Oakland, Calif.: Holmes Book Co., 1971.
Gold. Edited by James E. Sisson. Oakland, Calif.: Holmes Book Co., 1972. Written with Herbert Heron.

Autobiography

The Road. New York: Macmillan, 1907.
John Barleycorn. New York: Century, 1913.

Letters

Letters from Jack London. Edited by King Hendricks and Irving
Shepard. New York: Odyssey Press, 1965.

Additional Works

*Jack London Reports: War Correspondence, Sports Articles, and Miscel-
laneous Writings.* Edited by King Hendricks and Irving
Shepard. Garden City, N.Y.: Doubleday, 1970.
Jack London on the Road: The Tramp Diary and Other Hobo Writings.
Edited by Richard W. Etulain. Logan: Utah State Uni-
versity Press, 1979.
*No Mentor but Myself: A Collection of Articles, Essays, Reviews, and
Letters on Writing and Writers.* Edited by Dale L. Walker.
Port Washington, N.Y.: Kennikat, 1979.

Special Edition

Novels and Stories, Novels and Social Writings. 2 vols. The Library
of America. New York: Viking, 1982.

II. WORKS ABOUT JACK LONDON

Bibliographies

"Bibliographical Update." In *Critical Essays on Jack London*, ed-
ited by Jacqueline Tavernier-Courbin. Boston: C. K.
Hall, 1983.
Sherman, Joan. *Jack London: A Reference Guide.* Boston: G. K.
Hall, 1977.
Walker, Dale L., and James E. Sisson III. *The Fiction of Jack
London: A Chronological Bibliography.* El Paso: Texas West-
ern Press, 1972.

Woodbridge, Hensley C., John London, and George H. Tweney. *Jack London: A Bibliography*. Millwood, N. Y.: Kraus Reprint Corp., 1973.

Biographies

Barltrop, Robert. *Jack London: The Man, the Writer, the Rebel*. London: Pluto Press, 1976.
Hedrick, Joan D. *Solitary Comrade: Jack London and His Work*. Chapel Hill: University of North Carolina Press, 1982.
Kingman, Russ. *A Pictorial Biography of Jack London*. New York: Crown, 1979.
London, Charmian. *The Book of Jack London*. 2 vols. New York: Century, 1921.
London, Joan. *Jack London and His Times*. New York: Doubleday, 1939. Reissued with an introduction by the author. Seattle: University of Washington Press, 1968.
O'Connor, Richard. *Jack London: A Biography*. Boston: Little, Brown and Company, 1964.
Perry, John. *Jack London: An American Myth*. Chicago: Nelson Hall, 1981.
Sinclair, Andrew. *Jack: A Biography of Jack London*. New York: Harper and Row, 1977.
Stone, Irving. *Sailor on Horseback: The Biography of Jack London*. Cambridge, Mass.: Houghton Mifflin, 1938.
Walker, Franklin. *Jack London and the Klondike: The Genesis of an American Writer*. San Marino, Calif.: Huntington Library, 1966.

Books

Foner, Philip S. *Jack London: American Rebel*. New York: The Citadel Press, 1947.
Hendricks, King. *Jack London: Master Craftsman of the Short Story*. Logan: Utah State University Press, 1966.
Labor, Earle. *Jack London*. New York: Twayne, 1974.
McClintock, James I. *White Logic: Jack London's Short Stories*. Cedar Springs, Mich.: Wolf House Books, 1976.

Stoddard, Martin. *California Writers: Jack London, John Steinbeck, the Tough Guys.* New York: St. Martin's, 1983.

Walcutt, Charles Child. *Jack London.* Minneapolis: University of Minnesota Press, 1967.

Walker, Dale L. *The Alien Worlds of Jack London.* Grand Rapids, Mich.: Wolf House Books, 1973.

Watson, Charles N., Jr. *The Novels of Jack London: A Reappraisal.* Madison: University of Wisconsin Press, 1983.

Collections of Essays

Tavernier-Courbin, Jacqueline, ed. *Critical Essays on Jack London.* Boston: G. K. Hall, 1983.

Wilson, Ray, ed. *Jack London: Essays in Criticism.* Santa Barbara, Calif.: Peregrine Smith, 1978.

Selected Critical Articles, Notes, and Commentary

Ahearn, Marie L. "*The People of the Abyss*: Jack London as New Journalist." *Modern Fiction Studies* 22 (1976):73–83.

Baskett, Sam S. "A Brace for London Criticism: An Essay Review." *Modern Fiction Studies* 22 (1976):101–5.

_____. "*Martin Eden*: Jack London's Poem of the Mind." *Modern Fiction Studies* 22 (1976):23–26.

Beauchamp, Gorman. "Jack London's Utopian Dystopia and Dystopian Utopia." In *America as Utopia*, edited by Kenneth M. Roemer. American Cultural Heritage Series, No. 5. New York: Franklin, 1981.

_____. "Resentment and Revolution in Jack London's Sociofantasy." *Canadian Review of American Studies* 13 (1982): 179–92.

Beaver, Harold. "If Dogs Could Read." *New Statesman*, 31 March 1978, 438–39.

Blackman, Gordon N. "Jack London: Visionary Realist." *Jack London Newsletter* 13 (1980):82–95.

Brazil, John. "Politics and Art: The Integrated Sensibility of Jack London." *Jack London Newsletter* 12 (1979):1–11.

Brown, Deming, "Jack London and O. Henry." In *Soviet Atti-*

tudes Toward American Writing. Princeton, N.J.: Princeton University Press, 1962.

Bykov, Vil. "The Centennial of Jack London's Birth in the Soviet Union." *Jack London Newsletter* 10 (1977):7–10.

————. "Jack London in the Soviet Union." *The Book Club of California Quarterly News Letter* 24 (Summer 1959):52–58.

Campbell, Jeanne. "Falling Stars: Myth in 'The Red One.'" *Jack London Newsletter* 11 (1978):86–96.

Cooper, James G. "The Summit and the Abyss: Jack London's Moral Philosophy." *Jack London Newsletter* 12 (1979): 24–27.

————. "A Womb of Time: Archetypal Patterns in the Novels of Jack London." *Jack London Newsletter* 9 (1976):16–28.

Courbin, Jacqueline M. "Jack London's Portrayal of the Natives in His First Four Collections of Arctic Tales." *Jack London Newsletter* 10 (1977):127–37.

Dunford, Michael. "Further Notes on Jack London's Introduction to the Philosophy of Friedrich Nietzsche." *Jack London Newsletter* 10 (1977):39–42.

Flink, Andrew. "*Call of the Wild*: Jack London's Catharsis." *Jack London Newsletter* 11 (1978):12–19.

Forrey, Robert. "Jack London: The Cult and the Legend." *Modern Fiction Studies* 22 (1976):595–99.

————. "Three Modes of Sexuality in Jack London's *The Little Lady of the Big House*." *Literature and Psychology* 26, No. 2 (1976):52–60.

Franklin, Bruce H. "Jack London and Science Fiction." In *Future Perfect*. New York: Oxford University Press, 1978.

Gershenowitz, Harry. "The Natural History Controversy Between Theodore Roosevelt and Jack London: A Life Scientist's View." *Jack London Newsletter* 14 (1981):80–82.

————. "Richard Harding Davis and Jack London: An Ambivalent Friendship." *Jack London Newsletter* 13 (1980): 55–57.

Hensley, Dennis E. "Jack London's Alaskan Humor." *Pacific Historian* 21, No. 2 (1977):178–88.

————. "Jack London's Use of Maritime History in *The Sea Wolf*." *Pacific Historian* 23, No. 2 (1979):1–8.

Labor, Earle. "From 'All Gold Canyon' to *The Acorn Planter*:

Jack London's Agrarian Vision." *Western American Literature* 11 (1976):83–101.

_____. "Jack London, 1876–1976: A Centennial Recognition." *Modern Fiction Studies* 22 (1976):3–7.

_____. "Jack London's 'Planchette': The Road Not Taken." *Pacific Historian* 21, No. 2 (1977):138–46.

_____. "Jack London's Symbolic Wilderness: Four Versions." *Nineteenth Century Fiction* 17 (1972):149–61.

Lachtman, Howard. "Jack and George: Notes on a Literary Friendship." *Pacific Historian* 22, No. 2, insert (1978): 27–42.

_____. "Revisiting Jack London's Valley of the Moon." *Pacific Historian* 24, No. 2 (1980):145–56.

Lampson, Robin. "Some Sources of Jack London's Titles." *Pacific Historian* 20, No. 1 (1976):4–7.

May, Charles E. "'To Build a Fire': Physical Fiction and Metaphysical Critics." *Studies in Short Fiction* 15(1978):19–24.

Messenger, Christian. "Jack London and Boxing in *The Game*." *Jack London Newsletter* 9 (1976):67–72.

Mills, Gordon. "Jack London's Quest for Salvation." *American Quarterly* 7 (Spring 1955):3–14.

Naso, Anthony J. "Jack London and Herbert Spencer." *Jack London Newsletter* 14 (1981):13–34.

Orechwa, Olga. "Recent Soviet Publications Commemorating the Centennial of Jack London's Birth." *Jack London Newsletter* 9 (1976):78–80.

Oriard, Michael. "Jack London: The Father of American Sports Fiction." *Jack London Newsletter* 11 (1978):1–11.

Pankake, Jon. "Jake London's Wild Man: The Broken Myths of *Before Adam*." *Modern Fiction Studies* 22 (1976):37–49.

Peterson, Clell T. "The Jack London Legend." *American Book Collector* 9 (April 1959):15–22.

_____. "London and Lorenz: A Brief Note on Men and Dogs." *Jack London Newsletter* 12 (1979):46–49.

Qualtiere, Michael. "Nietzschean Psychology in London's *The Sea-Wolf*." *Western American Literature* 16 (1982):261–78.

Reich, Kenneth E. "Sport in Literature: The Passion of Action." *Jack London Newsletter* 12 (1979):50–62.

Ross, Dale H. "Jack London: An American Dilemma." *Journal of American Culture* 5, No. 4 (1982):57–62.

Rothberg, Abraham. "Land Dogs and Sea Wolves: A Jack London Dilemma." *Massachusetts Review* 21 (1980):569–93.

Shivers, Alfred S. "Jack London: Author in Search of a Biographer." *American Book Collector* 12 (March 1962):25–27.

Stasz, Clarice. "Androgyny in the Novels of Jack London." *Western American Literature* 11 (1976):121–33.

———. "The Social Construction of Biography: The Case of Jack London." *Modern Fiction Studies* 22 (1976):51–71.

Steed, D. "The Apocalyptic Structure of Jack London's *The Iron Heel*." *Jack London Newsletter* 13 (1980):1–11.

Stein, Paul. "Jack London's *The Iron Heel*: Art as Manifesto." *Studies in American Fiction* 6 (1978):77–92.

Suvin, Darko, and David Douglas. "Jack London and His Science Fiction: An Annotated Chronological Select Bibliography." *Science Fiction Studies* 3 (1976): 181–87.

Tambling, Victor R. S. "Following in the Footsteps of Jack London: George Orwell, Writer and Critic." *Jack London Newsletter* 11 (1978):63–70.

———. "A Nose for the King: Jack London's Version of a Korean Folk Story." *Jack London Newsletter* 14 (1981): 72–79.

Tavernier-Courbin, Jacqueline. "Jack London's Quest for the West." *Jack London Newsletter* 13 (1980):41–54.

Teich, Nathaniel, "Marxist Dialectics in Content, Form, Point of View: Structures in Jack London's *The Iron Heel*." *Modern Fiction Studies* 22 (1976):85–99.

Tierney, William. "Jack London's California Ranch Novels." *Pacific Historian* 21, No. 2 (1977):147–58.

Ward, Susan. Jack London and the Blue Pencil: London's Correspondence with Popular Editors." *American Literary Realism, 1870–1910* 14 (1981):16–25.

———. "Jack London as a Children's Writer." *Children's Literature: Annual of the Modern Language Association Seminar on Children's Literature and the Children's Literature Association* 5 (1976):92–103.

———. "Jack London's Women: Civilization vs. the Frontier." *Jack London Newsletter* 9 (1976):81–85.

———. "Social Philosophy as Best-Seller: Jack London's *The Sea-Wolf*." *Western American Literature* 17 (1983):321–32.

———. "Toward a Simpler Style: Jack London's Stylistic Development." *Jack London Newsletter* 11 (1978):71–80.

Watson, Charles N., Jr. "The Composition of *Martin Eden.*" *American Literature* 53 (1981):397-408.

_____. "Jack London: Up from Spiritualism." In *The Haunted Dusk: American Supernatural Fiction, 1820-1920*, edited by Howard Kerr, John W. Crowley, and Charles L. Crow. Athens: University of Georgia Press, 1983.

Whitfield, Stephen J. "American Writing as a Wildlife Preserve: Jack London and Norman Mailer." *Southern Quarterly* 15 (1977):135-48.

Wilcox, Earl. "'The Kipling of the Klondike': Naturalism in London's Early Fiction." *Jack London Newsletter* 6 (1973): 1-12.

Yoder, Jon A. "Jack London as Wolf Barleycorn." *Western American Literature* 11 (1976):103-19.

Index

206